BERLITZ®

SWEDEN

- A ✔ in the text denotes a highly recommended sight
- A complete A-Z of practical information starts on p.117
- Extensive mapping throughout: on cover flaps and in text

Printed in Switzerland by Weber SA, Bienne.

1st edition (1995/1996)

Although we make every effort to ensure the accuracy of the information in this guide, changes do occur. If you have any new information, suggestions or corrections to contribute, we would like to hear from you. Please write to Berlitz Publishing at the above address.

Text:	Doreen Taylor-Wilkie
Editors:	Donald Greig, Corinne Orde
Photography:	Bobby Andström
Layout:	Suzanna Boyle
Cartography:	Visual Image
Thanks to:	The Swedish Travel and Tourism Council, and particularly the various tourist boards around the country, for their invaluable assistance in the preparation of this guide. Thanks also to Jane Marquis in London for her help and humour.

Cover photograph: *Visby, in Gotland* © Bobby Andström
Photograph on page 4: *Seglora Kyrka in Skansen, Stockholm.*

CONTENTS

Sweden and the Swedes

Sweden is the largest and most prosperous of the three Scandinavian countries (Sweden, Norway and Denmark). This northern land is about the size of California, yet it is home to only around 8 million people, a figure which is comparable to the population of London. With miles and miles of beautiful empty countryside, it is sometimes called the Green Lung of Europe. To fly over it is to soar across tracts of endless green land and countless lakes, from the huge surfaces of Vänern and Vättern – which are more like inland seas – to thousands of smaller waters that peer up like sparkling eyes out of the forests.

Even the three largest cities in Sweden, Stockholm, Gothenburg (the Swedes call it Göteborg) and Malmö, have their own open spaces, and sometimes it is hard to believe that you are in what is technically an 'urban area'.

Roughly 15 percent of the country lies beyond the Arctic Circle, and the further north you travel the emptier the land becomes. To the east the great river Torneälven hugs the border with Finland. If the character of a nation is shaped by the landscape in which its people have lived for generations, then this is the land that has done so much to make the Swedes what they are today.

In 1991 the Swedish Social Democratic party lost heavily in the parliamentary elections for only the second time in 60 years, making way for a non-socialist coalition of Moderate, Centre, Liberal and Christian Democrat parties. The leader of the Moderates, Carl Bildt, became Prime Minister.

At the time, a British interviewer remarked: 'So, we're now seeing the end of the great Swedish welfare system?' In response to this the Swedish commentator simply laughed. 'You have to remember that this is only a change of emphasis,' she replied, 'we are not throwing out everything we've stood for overnight.'

Such a remark goes a long way to summing up Swedes and the Swedish way of life. (If the same question had been asked in another land, it might have elicited an impassioned defence.) This is a consensus society which discusses *ad nauseam*; one of the most frustrating answers when you try to reach a Swede on the telephone is the apology: 'Sorry, everyone's at a meeting.'

That meeting could be about almost anything, from a business or organizational decision to whether the office bicycle park should have more spaces or discussion of the current national issue – such as whether parents should be allowed to chastise their children physically (which is now forbidden) or whether to go ahead with the construction of a bridge between southern Sweden and Denmark (a debate which has dragged on for years). The essential thing is that everybody should have their say. On a larger scale, national or political issues are worked over in the same way, usually by a Commission, until an agreed view to which the majority of people can subscribe is absorbed into Swedish life.

At the root of this need for consensus is Sweden's closeness to its rural past, a life of small communities pulling together to survive the worst that nature could throw at them. It is hard to believe today, but only two or three generations ago, at the beginning of this century, Sweden's was still an impoverished rural society, with some 80 percent of the population scratching a living from the land.

Even then there were signs of the industrial success that was to follow. In barely one hundred years Sweden transformed itself into one of the world's richest countries, with a large number of people moving from outlying areas into the cities. Today, however sophis-

*L*illa Bommen, part of Gothenburg harbour, sends passengers and cargoes worldwide.

ticated Swedish city-dwellers may seem, their ties to the land, though often subconscious, are nonetheless strong.

Only Norway and Denmark can equal the Swedish passion for getting out into *the* nature (*naturen*). This emphasis on the definite article stems not just from translation, but also from the importance Swedes attach to the outdoors and all things natural. Whether it's summer or winter, they just love to go walking, skiing, climbing or, best of all, to immerse themselves in lake or sea.

Among the most popular pastimes are the late-summer expeditions into the forest to pick berries (something of a Swedish obsession), leaving a pleasing sensation that *the* nature has been used to good effect but has not suffered any damage. In the past, wild berries must have been a welcome addition to the diet. Today, the Swedes still use the traditional recipes but also serve berries in more sophisticated dishes – and store them in the deep freeze so that they can be enjoyed all year round.

7

*S*wedes love the natural fruits of the forests from unspoilt areas such as Värmland (right).

A very telling symbol of the speed of change in Sweden, and of how much the Swedes still cherish their rural memories, is the success story of the open-air museum. It started at Skansen in Stockholm as long ago as 1891, when the far-sighted Artur Hazelius, realizing the rapidity with which the **8** Industrial Revolution would transform Sweden, began to 'collect' characteristic buildings, bringing them in timber by timber from different areas and reassembling them in natural groups.

Today, communities everywhere have similar collections where, at weekends and holidays, ordinary citizens as well as hired workers don olden-day rural costume and play at being old-time craftspeople, demonstrating age-old skills or dancing the traditional dances to familiar fiddle tunes.

If all this makes the Swedes sound somewhat earnest and serious (which is undoubtedly the impression they can give), it is not a true picture – and certainly not a complete one. As with any nation the Swedes have their own private humour, and the best jokes about Sweden and the Swedes are often told by the locals themselves. Once things get going, however, Swedish reticence fades fast. For proof, try a crayfish party marking the start of the crayfish season in August. As the aquavit circulates, the laughter and arguments get louder.

Few communities can celebrate old rural festivals with as much zest. In cities, towns and villages people light bonfires on Walpurgis night, welcoming spring after the dark days of winter, paint their children's faces for Easter, dance round the midsummer Maypole, eat *surströmming* (pungent, fermented herring) or revel in the lovely candlelit celebration of Lucia in December – all quite unselfconsciously despite the Swedish reputation for reserve.

Externally, Swedes are not only taciturn but preserve a façade of satisfaction with all things Swedish – an attitude that often irks their Scandinavian neighbours. Such seeming arrogance, however, is no more than a hangover from the days of a rural, collective consciousness. Learn a little of the language and you'll be amazed at how critical of their government, political parties, modes and methods Swedes can be as the evening wears on.

*F*olk traditions linger in the province of Dalarna, where the people always dress for festivals.

Every nation has its taboos, however, and Sweden's is alcohol. Possibly as a result of a once strong teetotal movement, the concept of 'social drinking' (in the sense of going out for a quiet drink) has never really taken off, though Friday and Saturday revelling is cheerful enough. Once the top is off a bottle it rarely goes back on again, and even the ferocious prices, notably of spirits, seem a scant deterrent to over-indulgence. Indeed, one popular answer to this problem is to distil your own. So, if you're offered a novel brand of aquavit in an obscure bottle, just lift your glass and say *skål* ('cheers').

Then again, the Swedish attitude to sex is very relaxed. Four out of seven partnerships are unwed and divorce is common, but the sense of family is still strong. The typical image is of a laden family car setting off on a Friday evening for the *stuga* (wooden house) next to the lake or forest. With the influx into the cities earlier this century, old farms and small wooden buildings in the countryside were abandoned. They are much in demand again, and if he hasn't inherited a *stuga*, a Swede will build or buy one and spend as much time there as possible – swimming, sailing, fishing, working on the house or just enjoying the long summer evenings.

A Brief History

Pre-History, the Svear and the Vikings

Mention Scandinavia and most people think of the Vikings, who swooped into the world arena around AD 800 in a fierce rush of longboats against an unguarded shore, killing and plundering as they went.

Such is the conventional view, but Scandinavia actually reaches back 12,000 years, to when the last Ice Age retreated. A basin of glacier and sea was left behind as huge subterranean convulsions forced the earth upwards. By 2000 BC, the shape of the peninsula was much as it is today, and primitive hunters who had pushed north in the wake of the melting ice were now turning to farming and fishing.

During the Iron Age, independent tribes settled throughout the country, which came to be known as *Sverige*, or 'Land of the Svear', after the tribe on the shores of Lake Mälaren. Traces of these early Swedes are found all around the lake.

The majority of the Swedish Vikings went east rather than west. Their reasons for sailing were complex indeed, but foremost in their minds were certainly thoughts of exploration, trade and conquest. They sailed deep into what is now Russia,

*D*ecorated rune stones have long been a vital source of information about Viking times.

11

spreading south-east as far as Constantinople, where some joined the Imperial Guard. An Arab historian described them as 'great mustachioed angels, of evil disposition and smell'.

Much information about the early Svear has come to light through excavations at Birka, Sweden's first town (see p.32). At its height (in AD 800-975), Birka was the trading centre for a lakeside population of some 40,000 people, and now many graves and archaeological remains are dotted around Mälaren's shores. The Vikings are also recalled in tall rune stones decorated with a script that has long been decipherable. These are mostly around Lake Mälaren, Skåne, and the islands of Gotland and Öland, but one has been found as far north as Östersjön in Jämtland.

The Middle Ages

Christianity did not so much march into Sweden as slip in cautiously. In the 9th century the Frankish monk St Ansgar was allowed to preach to the people of Birka (see p.32), and

around AD 1000, Olof Skötkonung, the first Christian king of the Swedes, was baptized into the Byzantine Church (he had close ties with Constantinople). His sons Anund Jakob and Edmund supported Christianity, too, but did not succeed in bringing the Swedes to the new religion and ended by ruling only the area of Västergötland, in the south-west.

Around the mid-12th century, the pretender king Erik Jedvarsson (Erik IX, later St Erik, patron saint of the Swedes) was converted to Christianity, but only hesitantly did the Swedes give up the fierce paganism instilled by the Vikings.

Another strong medieval influence on Sweden was the German trading society – the Hanseatic League, or Hansa – which at that time controlled trade in most of northern Europe. The Hansa was well rooted in Sweden, particularly on the island of Gotland, and enjoyed good trade between the Baltic and Germany.

In the 13th century, Sweden was taking control of what later became Finland and there were

HISTORICAL LANDMARKS

c. AD 94	Roman historian Tacitus mentions *Svear*.
8th-11th century	Swedish Vikings range through Russia as far as Constantinople.
829-831	Ansgar tries to introduce Christianity.
993-1024	Reign of Olof Skötkonung, first Christian king of Sweden.
1150-1160	Erik Jedvarsson (St Erik) is baptized, spreads Christianity and captures Finland (1157).
12th century	Hanseatic League begins to dominate trade.
1397	Denmark, Sweden and Norway united.
1435	Meeting of the first Riksdag (Parliament).
1520	Stockholm Bloodbath.
1523	Gustav Vasa elected king and founds the Swedish nation state and the Vasa dynasty.
1527	Gustav Vasa imposes Reformation.
1611-32	Reign of Gustav II Adolf.
1718	Karl XII killed and Vasa dynasty ends.
1718-71	Age of Freedom; Riksdag gains in power.
18th century	Gustav III promotes culture and arts.
1808-09	Sweden loses Finland to Russia.
1810	French marshal Jean-Baptiste Bernadotte becomes Crown Prince.
1814	Danes cede Norway to Sweden.
1818	Crown Prince becomes King Karl XIV Johan of Sweden-Norway.
1880s-1890s	Industrial Revolution begins. Agricultural crisis leads to mass Swedish emigration.
1905	Norway gains independence.
1914-18	World War I; Sweden remains neutral.
1932	Social Democrats elected.
1939-45	World War II; Sweden declares neutrality.
1991	Sweden applies to join European Community. Elections won by non-Socialist coalition.

alternating periods of harmony and strife with Denmark. In 1397 Denmark, under the rule of forceful Queen Margareta, united the three countries by way of the Kalmar Union.

Alhough Denmark and Norway were to remain united until 1814, Sweden's membership did not last much longer than a stormy century. The country withdrew in 1523, with the accession to the Swedish throne of Gustavus I (Gustav Vasa).

The Kalmar Union brought to the fore Swedish men such as Engelbrekt Engelbrektsson, a minor noble who led a rebellion against Danish taxes in 1434, as well as Sten Sture, who changed Swedish history by defeating the Danish King Christian I at the Battle of Brunkeberg in 1471.

During its last 50 years, the Kalmar Union was anything but united and ended with the infamous Stockholm Bloodbath of 1520, when the Danish King Christian II held a feast for many of Sweden's greatest citizens and then executed 82 of them in Stockholm's Stortorget (see p.27).

The Royal Dynasties

From the early 15th century until the beginning of the 20th century, Sweden's history can be neatly divided into periods under different royal houses.

Gustav Vasa was in exile in Denmark when his father, two uncles and a brother-in-law were killed in the Stockholm Bloodbath. He hurried home to raise the country to arms and, once Sweden was freed, was elected King on 6 June 1523 (celebrated throughout Sweden now as National Day).

Vasa was a superb administrator and politician as well as a warrior. He harnessed the Hansa and reduced its power, cleverly manoeuvred the warring nobles and rich farmers, suppressed uprisings, and in 1527 implemented the Reformation, seizing control of the Church's lands and breaking its power and wealth over the next 15 years. (The first Swedish Bible appeared in 1541.) His aim was less religious than financial, for like King Henry VIII of England, he found the Church's riches extremely useful. (Monuments built by Gustav Vasa include the fortress-palaces at Vadstena, Uppsala and Gripsholm.)

His grandson, Gustav II Adolf, proved yet another brilliant warrior-statesman. During the Thirty Years' War, he crossed over the Baltic so successfully against Livonia (Estonia and Latvia), Russia and Poland that it became known as 'the Swedish Pond'. At home, he left affairs in the capable hands of his excellent Chancellor, Axel Oxenstierna, who owned Tidö Slott on Lake Mälaren's south side (see p.37).

King Gustav II Adolf was one of Sweden's greatest military geniuses and might have brought even more changes to the map of Europe, had he not been killed during the Thirty Years' War. He died at the age of 38 at the Battle of Lützen in 1632, in which Sweden beat the forces of the Holy Roman Empire. Like Gustav Vasa, he did much to open up Sweden, creating new towns, many in the north such as Umeå and Luleå (see pp.88 and 90), and his greatest memorial, Gothenburg (see pp.52-7).

King Gustav II Adolf was succeeded by his daughter, Kristina, then still a child, who abdicated in 1654 in favour of her cousin, Karl X. With him the Vasa dynasty's military genius flared again, albeit briefly, when he attacked Denmark in

This statue at Mora in Dalarna is one of many commemorating the great Gustav Vasa.

1658 in a daring raid over the ice, forcing the Danes to hand over what are now Skåne, Halland, Blekinge and Gotland.

In 1697, the boy-king Karl XII inherited a strong kingdom with many overseas possessions, but also a legacy of war. Indeed, the Swedes look on Karl XII as a romantic military hero. In reality, however, after storming across Europe successfully, his army was very near-ly wiped out by the Russians under Peter the Great in 1709 at the Battle of Poltava in the Ukraine. The 50,000-strong Russian army slaughtered the 20,000 Swedes, leaving only 1,500 to flee south to Turkey with the king. Karl spent five years in Turkey and then, in a 15-day endurance test, rode for 2,100km (1,300 miles) across Europe to return to Scandinavia. He was killed while fight-

Queen Kristina

The warrior king, Gustav II Adolf, raised his daughter Kristina as he would have a son. One commentator was to write: 'Science is to Kristina what needle and cotton are to other women.' She was only six when her father died at Lützen, and inherited the throne with the advantage of Gustav's formidable Chancellor, Axel Oxenstierna, as Regent.

Around the age of 16, Kristina began to attend her Council's meetings and by the time she became queen in 1644 she understood well the ways of government. She presided over a sumptuous baroque court, filled with brilliant young minds which could match hers in knowledge and wit, but later grew bored with her role as queen and quarrelled with her Chancellor. One possible reason for her abdication in 1654 was her increasing sympathy with the Roman Catholic faith, coupled with her reluctance to marry. She travelled to Rome, where she shocked her former subjects by announcing her conversion. Her response was: 'Men can never admire, never approve a deed which they themselves are incapable of performing.'

ing the Norwegians at Frederiksten fortress in Norway, just over the border from Bohuslän (see p.58) in 1718. He had not set foot in his capital city in 18 years, and his death ended not only the Vasa dynasty but Sweden's era as a great European power.

Freedom and Enlightenment

This was the beginning, however, of a great age of freedom, with the transfer of power from the monarch to the Riksdag (parliament). A Swedish talent for invention also began to emerge at this time, eventually leading to the practical industrial developments of the late 19th and early 20th centuries. Botanist Carl von Linné (Linneaus, 1707-78) published his definitive system for classifying plants, astronomer Anders Celsius (1701-44) invented the 100-degree thermometer, and there were several successful chemists such as CW Scheele (1742-86), who was the first to analyse the components of air as oxygen and nitrogen.

Liberty did not last long. Proud of being the first Swedish-born king since Karl XII, Gustav III ascended the throne in 1771 and moved steadily towards absolutism and autocratic rule. His most significant achievement was to found a native Swedish culture – indeed, his rule fell within the wider period known as the Gustavian Enlightenment. He ordered the building of Stockholm's Royal Opera House and Royal Dramatic Theatre, and transformed the theatre at Drottningholm Court into a showcase for Swedish talent.

King Gustav III was a fine writer himself and attracted men of letters to the Court, encouraging them by founding the Swedish Academies of Literature, Music, Art, and History and Antiquities.

For all his preoccupation with the arts and culture, the king could not ignore the wars with Russia that grumbled on periodically right up to the 19th century. Nor could his increasing autocracy fail to disturb the old noble families who felt their power slipping away to **17**

Gustav's more pliable favourites. The nobles plotted, with the result that Gustav's death could have been part of one of the operas he loved. He was assassinated at a masked opera ball – an event which was to inspire Verdi's opera, *Un Ballo in Maschera*.

Sweden's renowned botanist, Carl von Linné, is remembered at his museum in Uppsala.

The Making of Modern Sweden

As the Gustavian era faded away in rivalry and muddle, in 1808 Sweden lost Finland to Russia after a fierce two-year war. The first decade of the 19th century was marked by several great changes – in agriculture, constitution, foreign policy and, most noticeably at the time, dynasty. In 1810 the Riksdag, now with a written Constitution, invited a French marshal in Napoleon's army, Jean-Baptiste Bernadotte, to become Crown Prince. It was a strange choice – particularly since Bernadotte had at one time headed an army waiting in Denmark to invade Sweden – but one that proved justified. A firm hand was needed and the Swedes, who did not have confidence in Frederik VI of Denmark, the other main candidate for the position, found Bernadotte resolute in tackling the aftermath of the years of internal unrest.

Sweden's long struggle with Russia came to an end in 1809, with the surrendering of Finland to Tzar Alexander. Sweden then devoted the second half of the 19th century to internal development, a late industrial revolution, using its natural assets in mining, sawmilling and the manufacturing of wood-pulp, and promoting its successes in the inventive field, such as Alfred Nobel's dynamite and Gustav Pasch's safety match (see p.61). There was progress with the arrival of the co-operative movement, trade unionism and stirrings of the social democratic and women's movements.

Political problems nevertheless still demanded attention. In 1814 the Danes had handed Norway to Sweden, but the Norwegians objected and set up their own independent parliament. As a compromise, in 1818 the Crown Prince was crowned King Karl XIV Johan of Sweden-Norway. He was wise enough to rule gently, but a growing sense of national identity and a cultural renaissance led Norway along the road to statehood. Friction increased between the two countries until, in 1905, the union between Sweden and Norway came to an end.

In addition, a mounting agricultural crisis in the 1880s led to the emigration of what was eventually to be a total of more than one million people by the 1930s. So many Swedes settled in North America that some communities in Minnesota and Wisconsin subsequently spoke only Swedish for at least one generation. Today, these pioneers' descendants return in their thousands.

19

The 20th Century

Despite the successes of the 19th century – such as the establishment of a railway network, universal education and a good supply of raw materials – Sweden entered the 20th century a poor country, with 80 percent of the population involved in farming or rural industries. The Industrial Revolution brought poverty at first, but industrialization took hold rapidly so that during World War I, the demand for Swedish products reached a premium, bringing new-found hope.

No sooner were things picking up than the Great Depression which swept across most of the industrial world hit Sweden. The country was plagued by widespread bouts of unemployment. Strikes took place, leading to a tragic incident in which soldiers opened fire on several thousand demonstrators from Ångermanland, injuring many and killing five, including a woman bystander.

Political changes happened gradually, without any bloodshed, whilst the introduction of universal suffrage in 1921 completed a modern system of elections, political parties and fully democratic government. In the early years of the 1900s, the monarchy found itself under pressure with calls for the abdication of Gustav V. The king rode the storm, however, and emerged a popular ruler after World War I. His son, the present King, Carl XVI Gustav, has done much to ensure the monarchy's well-being.

This century has also been the era of social democracy and national neutrality, with Sweden taking part in neither World War, though she has since been active in the United Nations.

The Social Democrats have been in power for most of the last 70 years – even during periods of governments of Moderates, Liberals and Centre parties, the differences between left and right have not been split across the chasm of opposing ideologies found in many other countries.

Even the most dramatic and tragic recent event, the still-unexplained assassination of the Social Democratic Prime

Minister, Olof Palme, in 1986, did not lead to further bloodshed and instability. His death shook the nation's confidence and the international furore which followed indicated his stature as a world statesman.

Mounted police at Riksdagshuset (Swedish parliament), in Stockholm's Old Town.

Through its involvement with the United Nations and other organizations, Sweden plays a role far beyond its own borders, particularly with the establishment by businesses of links and satellite companies all over the world.

In 1991, the Social Democratic government applied to join the European Union (formerly European Community), a move which has since been backed by the present coalition government. Any final decision, however, will be subject, naturally, to a referendum. A 'yes' vote could see the course of Sweden's history undergoing another dramatic change. **21**

Where to Go

Sweden is the fourth largest country in Europe. Across 75 percent of the land the population density is only six people per square kilometre (15 per square mile), so there are long stretches between towns. It's better not to attempt to tackle the whole country in one visit.

We have divided Sweden into five main regions, each of which is subdivided according to old provincial names. These may not coincide with local government regions, but they are the names which are used by the Swedes themselves.

Stockholm

From any one of Stockholm's bridges it is easy to see that the Swedish capital is a city of sea and lake. Lake Mälaren in the west gives way to Saltsjön, the start of the Baltic Sea, in the east, and everywhere trees, gardens and buildings of mellow red stone and modern glass are never far from water.

The city covers 14 islands. At a time when water provided the easiest transport route, the small settlement where sea met lake quickly became the gateway to inland Sweden. Today, salt and freshwater are divided by the heavy lock gates of Slussen. Big Baltic ferries wait at the quays and, in summer, the bright sails of sailing boats scurry over the sparkling surface. Perhaps the most remarkable thing is that these waters are as clean as they look. Indeed, there are few capitals in the world where you can swim and fish for salmon right in the city centre.

The heart of the city is very compact and is best covered either on foot or, to start with, by sight-seeing boat from Stadhuskajen. The main areas are Gamla Stan (Old Town), Norrmalm, the modern business centre, Östermalm, an up-market residential suburb, Djurgården, Stockholm's outdoor playground, and Södermalm, literally the 'southern section'. Pleasant suburbs stretch along the water to the west and east, housing a significant portion

SWEDEN HIGHLIGHTS

Stockholm and Surroundings

Drottningholm Court Theatre, Royal Palace Grounds on Lovön in Lake Mälaren. By boat from Stadshuskajen. (See pp.28 and 31)

Djurgården, Stockholmers' outdoor playground with Skansen open-air museum. By boat from Slussen. (See p.29)

Hammarby, home of Carl von Linné (Linneaus), with a fine botanic garden. South of Uppsala. May- Sept. (See p.34)

The South

Bosjökloster, with a 12th-century church and *Ringsjön* bird lake. April-Oct 8am-8pm; at Höör, near Lund, Skåne. (See p.39)

Utvandrarnas hus, at Växjö, the largest European archive on emigration; tel. (0) 470-475-75 for opening times. (See p.48)

Gothenburg and the West

Trädgårdsföreningen. Glorious gardens, palm and butterfly houses, children's theatre – much more than a park. (See p.57)

Tanum's Bronze Age Carvings, best seen in the evening; tours run by *Vitlycke Hällristningsmuseum*; tel. (0) 525-209-50. (See p.57)

Håverud Aqueduct. The great 19th-century engineering feat on the Dalsland Canal, near the Håfreströmmen rapids. (See p.58)

The Central Heartlands

Midsummer celebrations at Rättvik and 'church-boats' on Lake Siljan. (See p.62)

Frösön Island, where the Viking drama/opera, *Arnljot*, is played out of doors in July. (See p.86)

Wild Bears at Sånfjället National Park. South of highway 84, north-west of Sveg in Härjedalen; tel. (0) 63-14-60-00. (See p.84)

Norrland and the Arctic

Midnight Sun over Lake Torneträsk. The unique phenomenon seen at its best. North of Kiruna on E10 to Abisko. (See p.95)

Ájte. Excellent museum in Jokkmokk offering a vivid portrayal of the Sami world and the 18th- and 19th-century settlers. (See p.94)

Arctic Hall. The world's biggest igloo, built each winter, lasts many weeks at Jukkasjärvi, 15km (12 miles) from Kiruna. (See p.96) of Greater Stockholm's population of around 1.5 million (only 700,000 live in the city itself). Beyond the suburbs are the alluring islands of Lake Mälaren to the west and the 24,000 islands of the *skärgård* (archipelago) to the east.

GAMLA STAN

What better place to start than Gamla Stan (Old Town), where Stockholm itself began its history over seven centuries ago?

Cross by the Riksbron (bridge) and your route will take you literally through the Swedish **Riksdagshuset** (the Parliament building), with its new wing glinting in the sun. Some time ago excavations revealed part of a medieval city here, below the Riksdag terrace. Part of the area has been turned into the **Medeltidsmuseet** (Medieval Museum), with the old wall and town gallows *in situ*.

You'll find everything from quirky statues to waterfront views in Sweden's beautiful capital.

Just beyond the Riksdag is **Kungliga Slottet** (the Royal Palace), with 608 rooms (one more, they say, than Buckingham Palace). The present building was built on the site of Tre Kronor (Three Crowns) Palace, which was razed by fire in 1697, and designed and started by Nicodemus Tessin, the Swedish royal architect, in 1646-81, then continued by his son and grandson. A visit here requires time since the palace (now no longer the royal family's main residence) houses no less than five separate museums and is famous for its Gobelin and Swedish tapestries.

Below the main building is the **Royal Armoury** with the stuffed horse and armour of the renowned warrior king, Gustav II Adolf. Also below ground are the **Crown Jewels**, beautifully lit and displayed in the

Skattkammaren (Royal Treasury). The Apartments of State and other rooms with magnificent interiors are open to the public, including **Oskar II's Writing Room**, full of 19th-century furniture and unaltered since the king's death in 1907. Each day in summer the Royal Guard parades gravely down Norrmalm's Hamngatan, over

*M*any cobbled streets in Gamla Stan connect leafy courtyards edged by old buildings.

the bridge to the palace for the Changing of the Guard at noon (1pm Sunday).

Right next to the palace is the **Storkyrkan** (Cathedral), a high-ceilinged Gothic building and Stockholm's oldest, dating from around 1250. Used as a parish church and for ceremonial occasions, it holds the famous statue of **St George and the Dragon**, a large wood-carving by Bernt Notke from 1489. Nearby, **Tyska Kyrkan**, the German Church, is almost as old, a reminder of the medieval German traders. Every four hours the bells of Tyska Kyrkan echo over Gamla Stan in two alternating hymn tunes.

At any time, people throng the shopping streets of Västerlånggatan and Österlånggatan. This is the area to wander, visiting spots such as **Mårten Trotzigs Gränd**, the narrowest street of all at the southern end of Västerlånggatan. More a stairway than a lane, it is less than one metre (3ft) wide.

At the centre of this tangle of streets is **Stortorget**, the square in which 82 Swedes were killed in the Stockholm Bloodbath (see p.14). Today a weekend market is held here. On one side is **Börsen** (Stock Exchange), where each year in an upstairs room the Swedish Academy picks the winner of the Nobel Prize for Literature.

Over a bridge to the west is **Riddarholmen** (Island of the Nobles), with the distinctive lattice-work spire of the 700-year-old **Riddarholmskyrka** (Church of the Nobility), where all the nation's monarchs since Gustav II Adolf (see p.15), who died in 1632, are entombed in fine sarcophagi.

NORRMALM

Norrmalm is the capital city's commercial, banking and business centre, with many hotels and restaurants, and famous stores such as NK and Åhléns (see p.98). Also here are the **Royal Opera House**, with its well-known Operakällaren restaurant and Café Operan (see p.79), and the **Kungliga Dramatiska Teatern**, where Max von Sydow and Greta Garbo, among others, made appearances early in their careers.

Although many older buildings survived the construction boom of the 1960s, some were replaced by modern blocks, and Norrmalm became all the poorer for it. The demolition process was stopped, however, when the Stockholmers rebelled and climbed the trees in **Kungsträdgården**, a pleasant square off Hamngatan, defying the men who had come to bulldoze the area. Thanks to them, Kungsträdgården remains the open-air heart of Norrmalm, with trees, flowers, games and small galleries. On one side, **Sverigehuset** (Sweden House) **27**

*H*umlegården is just one of the parks in Stockholm – a green space in summer, white in winter.

has a **tourist information office** and booking centre for excursions (see p.135).

A memorial to the period of demolition is **Sergels Torg**, a huge square with a giant glass obelisk at the top of Hamngatan. Opposite is the **Kulturhuset**, a modern arts centre and meeting place, while below the square is a lower level of walkways and covered shopping arcades, such as the **Gallerian**, which are ideal in winter.

For a taste of one of Stockholm's popular street markets, stroll along Sergelgatan and

past the glass skyscrapers to **Hötorget**, a typical, colourful fruit, flower and vegetable market. Here too is the **Konserthuset**, base of the Stockholm Philharmonic Orchestra and a venue for a variety of concerts, from classical to rock. In front of this fine building stands the lovely **Orpheus Fountain** – the work of Carl Milles, one of Sweden's most famous sculptors (see pp.32-33).

To the west, Norrmalm ends at Tegelbacken, with a good view of the **Stadshuset** (City Hall) on the next island of Kungsholmen. From any point in the south of the city it is hard to miss its massive square tower, 105m (450ft) high and topped with the golden Tre Kronor (three crowns) that are the city's symbol. Boats for Mälaren (see pp.31-3) depart from the quay below.

Inside, the Golden Hall – all marble and gilded mosaics – is the venue for the equally glittering Nobel Dance, while the Blue Hall, with its great staircase inspired by the Doges' Palace in Venice, is the scene of the Nobel Dinner.

DJURGÅRDEN

Djurgården ('deer park') was once a royal hunting ground and has retained much of its rural feel. From Nybroplan, at the foot of Hamngatan, you can reach the island on foot or by bus. The route passes through adjacent Östermalm, where fine old buildings line the Strandvägen waterside.

In summer, it is romantic to take the ferry from Slussen, which gives you a chance to see the harbour and the myriad small boats that sail out to the archipelago each weekend.

The short ferry trip takes you past a graceful boat, the *Af Chapman* (now used as a youth hostel), and the fortress island of Kastellholmen (used by the army).

Skeppsholmen, just behind Kastellholmen, is home to the **Moderna Museet** (Museum of Modern Art), which houses a fine 20th-century collection including works by Picasso and Warhol (the **Photography Museum** is here, too). Close by is the **Östasiatiska Museet** (Museum of Asian Art), with exhibitions of items that include a fine collection of Chinese art

---

Breaking the Language Barrier

Getting to grips with the Swedish language can take time. The following list of common words should be useful.

älv/ån	river	*öst*	east
berg, fjäll	mountain	*sjö/träsk*	lake
bro	bridge	*slott/hus*	castle
gata	street	*söder*	south
gränd	lane	*stad*	town
hamn	harbour, port	*strand*	beach
kyrka	church	*torg, plan, plats*	square
museet	the museum	*trädgården*	garden
nord	north	*väg/vägen*	road
ö or *holme*	island	*väst*	west

once belonging to King Gustav VI Adolf.

The northernmost of the islands (all linked by bridges), is Blasieholmen, now more a peninsula than the other two. Here you'll find the **Nationalmuseum** (National Museum of Art), with works by 16th- to 19th-century European masters, as

Carl Larsson's enchanting pictures were often based on the family life around him in Dalarna.

well as by the great Swedish painters Anders Zorn (see p.63) and Carl Larsson (see p.64).

As the ferry nears Djurgården the thrills and spills of the rides at **Gröna Lund**, a 19th-century amusement park, loom into view – among them the stomach-churning scenic railway and a traditional Ferris wheel. For the more discerning visitor, however, Djurgården means the Vasa Museum and Skansen (see below).

The **Vasa warship** was built as the pride of the fleet for

Gustav II Adolf, but, unfortunately, pride did indeed come before a fall. Top-heavy from the weight of her guns and decoration, the Vasa sank on her maiden voyage, drowning many on board before the eyes of the horrified monarch and the many Stockholmers who were there for the occasion.

She was discovered in the 1950s by a determined marine archaeologist, Anders Franzén, who salvaged her in 1961. Piecemeal restoration over 30 years has returned her to excellent condition and now, in a new museum, the Vasa is a magnificent sight, with several 'open' floors that reveal the structure from keel to decks.

Skansen, on the other hand, is out of doors, a re-created village where craftspeople display traditional skills. It is a place in which to linger and perhaps sample old sweets: try the delicious *bullar*, traditional and popular spicy buns.

This island playground also boasts two good museums. The **Nordiska Museet** (Nordic Museum) explains Nordic life from the 16th century on, with many specialized exhibitions, while the **Biologiska Museet** shows Nordic animals against dioramas to give the impression of a natural habitat.

There are various galleries here too, including the **Thiel Gallery**, once the collection of a Stockholm banker, and the delightful **Waldemarsudde**, former home of the so-called 'painter prince' Eugén, brother to Gustav V. This exquisite gallery, with fine gardens that run down to the water side, holds the Prince's whole collection – including several landscapes painted by his own hand.

LAKE MÄLAREN AND THE ARCHIPELAGO

Lake Mälaren stretches 100km (70 miles) west of Stockholm and has innumerable enticing islands. A good day out is by vintage steamer to Drottningholm on Lovön (some 50 minutes from Stadshuskajen).

Lovön has long been a royal island. **Drottningholm Palace**, built in the 17th century and now the royal family's main home, has a wonderful garden, **31**

a smaller version of Versailles. Most popular is **Drottningholm Court Theatre**, built in 1766 by Queen Louisa Ulrika, the mother of Sweden's great patron of the arts, Gustav III. He encouraged theatre and arts of every variety and his reign became a Golden Age (see pp.17-18). The graceful little theatre flourished and served to entertain the Royal Court, which also amused itself in both the **Kina Slott** (Chinese Palace) and its grounds nearby.

All this ended when Gustav III was assassinated, fittingly, at a masked ball. The Court Theatre was shut and forgotten until the 1920s, when Professor Agne Beijer pushed open the door and, to his astonishment, found the 18th-century theatre, preserved undamaged.

In summer, opera and ballet are performed here, or you can accompany daily guided tours of the theatre, complete with original backdrops and 18th-century equipment. If you're at a performance, note the court officials' names, which are still discernible on the seat backs. (Tickets are sold at the kiosk

Drottningholm Palace – an idyllic home on Lake Mälaren for the Swedish Royal Family.

on Norrmalmstorg, which will also provide details of events at many Stockholm venues.)

Further west is the island of **Björkö**, with the remains of Sweden's oldest settlement, the Viking **Birka**. Archaeological digs have shown that from AD 800 to 975 Birka was a trading centre of 40,000 people on the shores of Lake Mälaren. In those days nothing divided the lake from the Baltic Sea, and travellers sailed in from Russia and Arabia. It was then that St Ansgar, a Frankish monk, arrived from Europe to convert the local tribes (see p.12). The chapel on Björkö, built in the 1930s, is dedicated to him.

East of the city centre are the inner islands of the archipelago, which are best seen on an excursion that lasts about seven hours. In summer, water sets the mood for Millesgården, the summer home of sculptor

Carl Milles (1875-1955), on **Lidingö**. Here he reproduced the statues that had made him famous. Set on steep terraces, the figures seem to fly, almost defying gravity.

Although close to the city, the **Fjäderholmarna** (Feather Islands) form a genuine archipelago. These rocky, tree-covered islets have an aquarium of Baltic fish, a smoke-house and an archipelago museum.

Vaxholm is a great place for watersports. The **Fortress** at Vaxholm dates from the 16th century and was built to guard Stockholm's main sea route. Vaxholm now has more peaceful purposes – with the **Homestead Museum**, housed in a fishing cottage, the old **Customs House**, as well as special Herring Picnics at the fortress (included in one of the tours).

Two or three hours into the Baltic is a well-known summer haunt, **Sandhamn** on **Sandön**, a village with sandy beaches. Seafarers from many lands rest peacefully in its cemetery, and the **Sandhamns Värdshus** restaurant has been feeding sailors ever since 1672.

33

Stockholm's Surroundings

UPPSALA

Stockholm sits south of Uppland, on the border between Södermanland and Uppland. This area includes the old capital of **Uppsala**, which saw the last days of heathen Sweden.

Today, Uppsala is the seat of Sweden's Archbishop and can boast Scandinavia's largest **Gothic Cathedral**. Here, too, is Sweden's oldest university, which ensures a lively student life around the narrow streets. Students once gathered in the **Anatomical Theatre** to watch operations being performed.

Famous alumni of the university include Carl von Linné (Linnaeus), botanist, and Dag Hammarskjöld, a great poet, peacemaker and former Secretary General of the United Nations. Carl von Linné's legacy is the **Linnéträdgården** (Linné Gardens), a beautiful oasis of plants. His summer home, **Hammarby**, has a small but fine botanic garden.

The city is dominated by its **Castle**, a brick fortress where Gustav II Adolf held talks that plunged Sweden into the Thirty Years' War (see p.15) and where Queen Kristina gave up her crown (see p.16).

Off the E4 route to Uppsala from Stockholm are the ruined monasteries of **Sigtuna**, while further north, in a cluster of lakes, you will find **Skokloster**, the seat of the Wrangles, an important family that once ruled much of Scandinavia. Today their great white house, with a large collection of 17th-century weapons and a motor museum, is open to the public.

AROUND THE LAKE

Leaving Stockholm on the E20/E4 on Mälaren's southern side, the first stop is the idyllic small town of **Mariefred** – which can also be reached by steamship from Stadshuskajen. This is a typical lakeside town with 14th-century **Gripsholm Slott**, once owned by Gustav Vasa. Gripsholm's royal portraits are quite compelling, and a small theatre goes back to

the days of that royal patron of the arts, Gustav III (see p.17). Another delight is the **Östra Södermanlands Järnväg** (the East Södermanland Railway), a superb steam railway between Mariefred and Läggesta 4km (2½ miles) away.

West from Gripsholm, 17th-century **Sundbyholm** has been turned into a hotel and restaurant, from where **Sigurdsristningen**, an ancient rock carving, is a short walk through the beech woods.

Eskilstuna goes back to the great days of steel and iron, and the **Rademacher Smithies**, founded in 1658, are now an industrial museum. The city also has a popular zoo park, with a pride of white tigers.

From Eskilstuna retrace the road back to the pretty little town of **Strängnäs** to see the vast **Gothic Cathedral**. From here, head north by route 55 – over bridges and islands – to

Grispholm Slott was once owned by Gustav Vasa, who had a taste for fine castles.

Lake Mälaren's northern bank. A side road west leads to the ancient estate of **Ängsö Slott**, full of old legends, on its own island of **Ängsö** – a good place for swimming, fishing, canoeing and walking – and you'll also find a campsite there.

Heading west on the E18 you come to **Västerås**, an early trade centre, whose **Cathedral** holds the tomb of Erik XIV. Not far away, **Anundshög** has Sweden's largest Iron Age burial mounds and ship tumuli. Västerås is also a pleasure sailing centre and is linked to the capital by ferry.

South of Västerås, the 17th-century **Tidö Slott** was the home of Axel Oxenstierna, the great Swedish Regent who ruled during the minority of Gustav II's daughter, Kristina (see p.16). Today, Tidö houses a **Toy Museum** with some 35,000 items, and the grounds are home to hundreds of deer.

Close to the western end of Lake Mälaren is another castle, **Strömsholm Slott**, which was once a royal residence. There is an excellent riding centre with a carriage museum here.

Watersports enthusiasts should head towards **Kolbäcksån** and, close by, the **Strömsholm Canal**. At the end of the lake, where the road joins the E20 from the south side, is **Arboga**, which has some of the best preserved buildings in Sweden. In 1435 this town was the meeting place for what later becamei Sweden's first Riksdag (parliament) and for the election of Engelbrekt Engelbrektsson to the position of Captain of the Realm (see p.14).

West, the land rises into the mountainous area of Bergslagen, where the birthplace of Swedish steel, **Örebro**, sits at the western end of Lake Hjälmaren. Örebro also has a fine castle and is the main town of Sweden's smallest province, Närke. Three places recall mining days: the old **Strassa Gruvor** (mines) allow visitors to travel underground in original mining carts; at **Lilla Nora**, wooden houses form a well-preserved 19th-century village where the steel workers lived; whilst **Siggebohyttan**'s manor house gives a taste of how the rich mill-owners once lived. **37**

The Smiling South

The south of Sweden between the Kattegat and the Baltic has a character of its own, shaped by both history and proximity to Continental Europe (it was from the coast here that Karl X Gustav sent his troops across the ice to Denmark in 1657; see p.45). It is also mellowed by a warmer climate and made cosmopolitan by its role as a summer playground.

SKÅNE

Thanks to its fertility, Skåne is known as 'Sweden's Granary'. The province is somehow different from the rest of Sweden. Even the accent has a hint of Danish, which is no surprise as it's only a 25-minute boat trip from the old port of Helsingborg to Helsingör in Denmark.

Skåne has Sweden's richest farms set in a landscape of rich colour. The magnificent coastline offers beaches, fishing villages, skerries for sea-fishing and, on the **Bjäre Peninsula** to the north-west, rocks shaped like statues at **Hovs hallar**. To the west of Skåne is the south's most fashionable resort, **Båstad**, which is known for its international tennis events.

*F*alsterbo in the far south-west is a typical example of the coast's fine bathing beaches.

Torekov, a fishing village at the tip of the Bjäre peninsula, has retained its old identity. From here it's a short trip by boat to **Hallands Väderö**, an island nature reserve harbouring some interesting birdlife and flora. Many coastal stretches are a bird-watcher's paradise, and there are also several good bird lakes inland, such as **Ringsjön**, north-east of Lund.

The south's long-established wealth is reflected in over 250 castles and historic buildings. A good example, standing on an island in Lake Ringsjön, is **Bosjökloster**. Dating from about 1080, this former Benedictine convent boasts a fine 12th-century church, fine gardens and parkland, as well as a thousand-year-old oak tree and a small zoo.

Local colour: from the historic fortress of Glimmingehus (above) to brilliant poppy fields (right).

In addition, many towns are fortified – Helsingborg's medieval keep, **Kärnan**, the only one of its kind in Sweden, is just one example. **Landskrona**, further south has **Citadellet**, which dates from 1549.

For some fine scenery, follow the southwestern peninsula of **Österlen** – you can stay at its two friendly summer resorts, **Falsterbo** and **Skanör**.

Ferry routes link **Trelleborg**, on the south coast, to the German ports of Travemunde, Rostock and Sassnitz. Further on, **Ystad** boasts rare old houses in a near-Tudor style, and is also the ferry departure point for the Danish isle of **Bornholm**. To the east, the tall rock of **Stenshuvudet** rises majestically from the Baltic above a landscape that contains more fruit-farms and orchards than any other part of Sweden.

Another great fortification from the early wars is the 15th-century **Glimmingehus**, southwest of **Simrishamn**, which is regarded by some as Scandinavia's best preserved medieval fortress. Some of these old buildings are now hotels; others are used for folk dancing and cultural events.

Malmö and Lund

Malmö, south of Helsingborg on the west coast, is a rare mixture of old and new with just under 250,000 citizens. Like most ports, the influence of immigrants from many parts of the world has given it a cosmopolitan, jaunty air – one in five Malmö residents has a foreign background. The renowned film-maker Ingmar Bergman was once the director of the theatre here.

Stortorget (central square) is huge, and has a fine **Rådhus** (City Hall). Here too is one of the earliest houses in Malmö, **Jorgen Kockshus**, which dates from the early 16th century. Just off the square to the east is the lovely, 14th-century **St Petri's Kyrka**, replete with treasures from the 16th and 17th centuries. Danish king Kristian III built **Malmöhus**, now a museum, when Skåne was still part of Denmark.

The Malmö **tourist office**, north of Stortorget and opposite the Central Station, runs guided tours, and public bus no. 20 is equipped with information to help visitors pinpoint sights. For a restful break, try **Pildammsparken**, Sweden's largest landscaped park, whose amphitheatre is used for summer performances.

The **Konserthuset** is the base of the Malmö Symphony Orchestra. In August, the big

*F*ruit, flowers and vegetables scent the air at Möllevångstorget, Malmö's best street market.

Malmö Festival attracts large crowds, as does the nearby **Jägersro**, Sweden's only combined trotting and race track and the venue for the Swedish Derby, also in August.

Lund, 27km (19 miles) or so north-east of Malmö, is a gracious university city whose **42** winding, cobbled streets and old buildings create an atmosphere of age and learning. It is believed to have been founded by Danish King Sven Tveskägg ('Fork beard') in 990, and in 1020 his son King Canute began to turn it into a political, cultural, commercial and religious centre. By 1103 it had become the seat of the Archbishop of all Scandinavia and Finland. Lund's towering Romanesque **Cathedral**, which was consecrated in 1145, has a fine altarpiece dating from the 15th century. Its **Astronomical Clock** shows the movement of the heavenly bodies, the paths of the sun and moon and, for good measure, the journey of the three wise men to Bethlehem when it chimes.

Lund University, which was founded in 1666, is set in beautiful gardens with a big stone fountain. Its 30,000 students form an important part of Lund's modest population of 90,000, particularly on special occasions such as Walpurgis night (see p.102).

Lund has good museums; worth visiting are the **Lunds Konsthall** (Art Gallery) and the **Historiska Museet** and the **University Library**, as well as the **Kulturhistoriska Museet** (Museum of Cultural History).

BLEKINGE

The Swedish writer Selma Lagerlöf (see p.60) described Blekinge as the land of three steps – coast, inland and forest – and today it is known as 'Sweden's Garden'. It has a string of small towns with long histories and a lovely archipelago with countless islands. Inland, the forest acted once as a refuge for outlaws from the border wars and is dotted with small, well-concealed villages. This miniature province is in fact something of a microcosm of Sweden – right down to its famous salmon river and good golf course.

Blekinge's largest town, 17th-century **Karlskrona**, has had a long association with the Swedish Navy. Its wide streets, old buildings and fortresses have a flavour of the sea – not least because it is built on 30 islands – and it offers excellent facilities for boating, fishing and swimming. **Marinmuseet** (the Maritime Museum) has a splendid collection of ships' figureheads, and the training ship **Jarramas** can be seen tied up at one quay.

On the E22 into Blekinge from Skåne in the west, small towns are found mostly on, or near, the coast. The exception is **Olofström**, 30km (21 miles) north on the Skåne border. This has a 19th-century spa, **Jämsög**, close by, and an interesting old water and saw mill on **Lake Halen**, which is also good for bathing.

43

*B*ikes at Kalmar's Domkyrka (cathedral): Swedes are environmentally conscious – and fit!

Close to the coast of Blekinge are a number of towns. In medieval **Sölvesborg** are the ruins of **Sölvesborg Slott**, a castle from the 13th century, and **Mörrum** (on the **Mörrumsån**, a superb salmon river) attracts anglers from near and far. **Karlshamn** is notable for its **Emigrants' Monument**, a moving tribute to those who left their homes for a brave

new world across the ocean (see p.19), while **Ronneby**, a 19th-century spa, is now Sweden's biggest conference and recreation centre.

SMÅLAND

Fly from Stockholm to the east coast city of Kalmar and you will see Småland as a map of green forest studded with hundreds of small blue lakes and lighter patches that are fields and villages. Driving along the roads through those forests, the pine and birch stands open out into moorland and small towns. Småland has always been an area of smallholdings where 'crofters' lived off an ungrateful soil, and it has bred a tough, determined people.

The province has given birth to many of Sweden's notable figures, including the Father of Botany, Carl von Linné (Linneaus), tennis players Mats Wilander and Stefan Edberg, soprano Jenny Lind (the 'Swedish Nightingale') and writer Astrid Lindgren (see p.46).

From Småland also came the majority of the one million

people (around one-quarter of Sweden's population at that time) who sailed to the New World (see p.19), and even to-day Småland celebrates Minnesota Day in August.

Kalmar is an ancient city, first noted on an 11th-century rune stone, and the formidable 12th-century **Kalmar Slott** has long guarded the straits between the mainland and Öland. The castle's red-stone battlements, its round towers and moat are still as imposing as they were in 1397, when the Kalmar Union was signed here (see p.14). Kalmar was also one of the trading ports of the powerful German Hanseatic League (see p.12).

Kalmar Slott is now the last resting place of what remains of the royal ship *Kronan*. In May 1676, when Sweden was at war against a Danish-Dutch fleet, Admiral Lorentz Creutz was tucking into a substantial

---

A Daring Raid

Until 1658 the border between the provinces of Blekinge and Småland was Sweden's uneasy frontier with Denmark. Marked by the small community of Kristianopel, once a Danish fortress, the area was fought over for centuries. Then, the icy winter of 1657-58 gave Sweden's King Karl X Gustav his chance …

Arctic weather froze the sea between Sweden and Denmark and the Great Belt separating Denmark's first and second islands. Although already at war with Poland and Russia, Karl Gustav sent his troops on to the ice. Two squadrons of horses and riders fell through and drowned, but 5,000 foot soldiers and 1,500 cavalry reached Denmark's central island, Fyn.

Despite a thaw, they followed that journey with an even more hazardous crossing to Denmark's main island, Sjælland (Zealand), and reached the walls of Copenhagen. Denmark had no choice but to agree to the Treaty of Roskilde and cede to Sweden its northern provinces on the mainland. They have remained Swedish ever since.

Astrid Lindgren and Pippi Longstocking

Astrid Lindgren, author of *Pippi Långstrump*, was born in 1907 in Vimmerby in north-east Småland, which has now become almost a place of pilgrimage for both children and parents.

Astrid Lindgren did not plan to sell her writing. She first made up the stories for her young daughter, telling her of the adventures of Pippi Longstocking, a small girl who was full of charm but lonely. Once published, however, these enchanting tales quickly became favourites in more than 30 languages.

Astrid Lindgren has written some 50 books, but no character has become as popular as the original Pippi. Her success was such that, in 1976, the Swedish authorities assessed her taxes as 102 percent of her income! The result was a rare move by Lindgren into adult fiction with a rapier-sharp satire on the bureaucracy of an 'imaginary' dictatorship.

lunch when news was brought that the enemy was close by. The admiral turned his ship to engage the enemy but turned too swiftly. The sails plunged sideways, water gushed in and something fired the magazine. The blinding explosion blew out one side of the vessel and, of the crew of 842, only 42 souls survived.

A diving team found the *Kronan* in 1980, since when its treasures have gradually been retrieved, including the ship's bell, cannon and compass and some 300-year-old brandy.

The northern archipelago referred to as the **Blue Coast**, where Småland shades into Östergötland, offers fishing villages, beaches and hundreds of islands and harbours for all kinds of watersports. **Västervik**, 130km (90 miles) north of Kalmar, is an excellent starting-point for deep-sea fishing and has a popular **Ballad Festival** during the summer. Ferries to Gotland leave from here and from Oskarshamn, the main terminal further south.

Heading inland on Highway 33 from Västervik will bring

you to **Vimmerby**, birthplace in 1907 of the much-loved children's writer, Astrid Lindgren. Celebrating her works here is **Saga Town**, which consists of miniature buildings, all authentic copies of the places she wrote about. They offer an excellent introduction to her characters and stories.

The Kingdom of Glass

Away from the coast and hidden in the forests is Småland's most famous industry. Ranging from the small glassworks at **Pukeberg** to such famous names as **Kosta** and **Orrefors**, 17 highly profitable glassworks lie near the 80km (50-mile) stretch of Highway 25 between Nybro and Växjö.

As well as building Kalmar Slott, in 1556 King Gustav Vasa brought some glass-blowers to Sweden, but another 200 years were to pass before glass came to Småland. The province had wood for the furnaces and, in 1742, when Karl XII rewarded two of his generals with the governorship of Småland, they set up the first glass-

works. Taking the first syllables of their surnames (Anders KOskull and Georg Bogislaus STAel von Holstein), *Kosta* was born. Today, most companies welcome visitors to watch the skill that turns a glowing mass of molten glass into exquisite shapes, and most have a shop selling glass at bargain prices. Some will also arrange special Hyttsil Evenings (see p.113-14), which hark back to the days when herring was cooked in the heat from the furnaces.

T ransluscent and ethereal – an exhibition of designer glass made by Orrefors in Småland province. **47**

Another industry that owes its lifeblood to this area is furniture-making. Much of the furniture that is bought in the distinctive IKEA stores all over Europe comes from Småland.

In **Växjö**, to the west of the glass country, there is a good **Glasmuseet** (Glass Museum) – but its main claim to fame is the **Utvandrarnas hus** (House of the Emigrants), which holds the largest archive on emigration in Europe. One of its founders was Vilhelm Moberg, author of *The Emigration Trilogy*, the best work on the great exodus, which was later made into two films.

North-west of Växjö, not far from the border with Halland, **Värnamo** has an **Open Air Museum** with a collection of old buildings. Approximately 25km (18 miles) further on, near **Anderstorp**, you reach Småland's version of the Wild West at the **High Chaparral**, a ranch-style park located out in the forests. At its northernmost tip the most fertile area of this large province stretches as far as the southern end of Lake Vättern (see p.59).

THE ISLANDS

The two south-eastern Baltic islands, **Öland** and **Gotland**, are very different in style and character both from the mainland and each other. Öland is long and narrow, connected to Kalmar on the mainland by Europe's longest **bridge**, with slender arches stretching for just over 6km (almost 4 miles), while Gotland, 120km long and 40kmat its widest (90 by 30 miles), is the Baltic's largest island. Gotland claims the longest hours of sunshine in Sweden – over 500 from 15 June to 15 August.

Öland

The remarkable bridge that stretches between the mainland and Öland transports you to a different scene altogether. Öland is its own world, with the huge limestone plateau of **Alvaret** – a botanist's dream with wild flowers galore that include 40 species of orchid.

Borgholm, the first town over the bridge, and **Borgholm Slott**, are worth lingering over.

Öland Zoo, lying just below the bridge, has long been patronized by the Royal Family, who stay on Öland at **Solliden**, their summer home.

Above all, this is an outdoor island – and birding country. Visit **Ottenby Observatory** at the southern tip of the island, next to **Långe Jan**, Sweden's tallest lighthouse. Ottenby is popular with bird watchers on account of the migrants, such as honey buzzards, which can sweep past in huge numbers.

In prehistoric times people lived in the safety offered by the island, although only their burial grounds remain now. Of great interest is the fortified village of **Eketorp**, which has been restored to show the life of a busy community between AD 300 and 1300. The ruined

The great bridge to Öland from the mainland offers wonderful views of water and islands.

walls of **Gråborg Castle**, 8.5m (25ft) high and in places almost as wide, hint at the size of this 6th-century fortress.

Gotland

The first modern outsiders to discover Gotland were writers and artists such as Strindberg, Selma Lagerlöf and Carl Larsson. Gotland is often called the *Island of Roses and Ruins*, thanks partly to its deep red roses, which are in bloom as late as November. Everything grows here, and **Almedalen**, the former Hanseatic harbour,

in Visby is now a lovely garden park with graceful plants in reed-lined pools. In summer the modern harbour is filled with masts, while boat-owners lounge in outdoor cafés.

Visby was once an important trading centre in the Hanseatic period (see p.12), the German legacy of which shows in the town's architecture. In total, 3km (2 miles) and 44 towers remain of the medieval walls. By sad contrast, the Gothic **St Catherine's Church** is now a ruin beside the market square.

Within the old walls, much of the medieval city still stands

– step-gabled houses with red pantile roofs, narrow streets, buildings like **Gamla Apotek** (chemist's shop), which now sells silverware, and the three towers of **Domkyrkan Sita Maria** (the cathedral).

Gotland still possesses 90 medieval churches, a tribute to the wealth of the farmers in the years before Visby gained the trade monopoly. Every year in August, Medeltidsveckan (Medieval Week) turns back time when Gotlanders don medieval costumes to revel as merchants, monks and high-born ladies.

Like Öland, Gotland offers outdoor attractions. The largest forest, Lojstaskogen, still has a wild herd of an unusual breed of ponies with two toes, called *Russ* since they are believed to have come from Russia (*Ryssland* in Swedish). There are also two good bird islands just south of Visby.

North of Visby, one of the island's best sights is found at **Lummelundagrottorna**: magnificent limestone caves with huge stalactites.

Fårö, a small island off the north of Gotland, is a military zone, but it has been open to foreigners since 1992 (with the exception of its southernmost tip). From Rute in Gotland visitors must proceed straight through to Fårö Church, but can then wander freely around the old village. You will also be able to see the *Raukar* stone formations here.

*V*isby (left), with its powerful walls still intact, is a fine setting for Medieval Week (below).

Gothenburg and the West

The most exciting way to arrive in Gothenburg is by sea, standing on deck as the land creeps towards you. The ship heads through a maze of small islands and into the mouth of the Götaälv, past the ruins of Elfsborg Fortress, which once guarded this entrance. Ahead is the high curve of the Älvsborg Bridge; at night the scene glints and glows with lights.

Sweden's largest passenger and cargo harbour is transited by some four million travellers each year. It is changing, too, since many of the shipyards that closed in recent years are now being redeveloped.

The most obvious feature is the **Skanskakrapan**, an office tower that looms over everything like a giant red and white funnel. On the 22nd floor the **Utkiken** ('lookout') provides spectacular views of the city. On the other side of Lilla Bommen Hamn is the new **Göteburgsoperan** (Opera House), opened in 1994.

Houses are also starting to rise close to the water and the harbour is becoming a popular place to live. Along the south bank at **Packhuskajen**, vintage ships herald a **Sjöfartscenter** (Maritime Centre), which will eventually see 20 historic vessels moored at the dock. It will be part of the **Sjöfarts Museet** (Maritime Museum), which is sited further down river in the **Masthugget** area. From the water the museum is picked out easily – in front stands a tender statue of a sailor's wife gazing out to sea on the 44m (142ft) **Sjöfartstorne** tower.

GUSTAV ADOLF'S CITY

Gothenburg was founded in 1603 by Karl IX, by what was then Sweden's only outlet to the western sea. The city huddled around Älvsborg Fortress, but this was captured by the Danes in 1612 during the Kalmar War. They ransomed it for one million Riksdalers, a huge sum that led to heavy taxes and took over six years to pay, by which time the town had almost crumbled away.

The city was founded for a second time in 1619 by Karl IX's son, Gustav II Adolf, and it is he who is commemorated by a statue in the square that bears his name, **Gustav Adolfs Torg**. There he stands, pointing imperiously to the place where his new city was to rise, south of the Götaälv.

Gustav saw Gothenburg as Sweden's western trading gateway and he enlisted Dutch builders, who designed a layout with moat and canals. Two canals remain to give the city its characteristic style, which is best seen by **Paddan Boat** (quite literally 'Toad Boat') from Kungsportsplatsen.

Little of Gustav Adolf's city survived the fury of the periodic fires that razed the wooden buildings, and today Gothenburg is a fascinating jumble of dates and styles. The surviving buildings from those early days are all stone-built: the **Kronhuset**; part of the old wall, Bastion Carolus Rex at Kungsgatan; and the **Skansen Lejonet** and **Skansen Kronan** forts, the latter in the city's earliest suburb, Haga, just over 2km

(1½ miles) from the centre and now filled with military artefacts. The city remains compact though, easy to see by foot, tram or bus.

The Dutch-style Kronhus was built in the 1640s as the city armoury. In 1660 it briefly became the House of Parliament, when Karl X Gustav died suddenly in the city and his four-year-old son came to the throne as King Karl XI. It is now the **Stadsmuseet** (or City

Museum). In 1759 two rows of buildings were erected next door as workshops for the city artillery, and today they form the **Kronhusbodarna**, turn-of-the-century workshops where you can buy craftware, test the aroma of spice or nibble tasty old-fashioned cakes and buns.

On the west side of Gustav Adolfs Torg is the **Rådhuset** (City Hall), from 1672, and to the north **Börsen**, the old Stock Exchange. The first of the big canals, **Stora Hamn Kanalen**, runs past the southern edge of the square, with fine mercantile buildings along its banks. On the north (Norra Hamngatan) is **Ostindiska Huset**, the Swedish East India Company's premises, now home to three museums, including the **Historiska Museet** (Gothenburg from the Middle Ages to the start of this century).

In contrast to all this history, north-east of Gustav Adolfs

There is plenty of opportunity for messing about by (or on) the river and canals in Gothenburg.

Torg is **Nordstan**, Sweden's largest shopping centre. An arcade now covers the old central street, leading to Central Station and the bus terminus.

WALKING DOWN THE AVENUE

Avenyn (Kungsportsavenyn) is more like a French boulevard than a Swedish street. Lined with trees, shops and cafés spilling on to the wide pavements, it is always full of people – musicians, vendors, or locals just out for a stroll and a chat. It starts at busy **Kungsportsplatsen** with a statue of Karl IX standing before the main **Tourist Office**.

Crossing over the second of Gothenburg's two canals, **Rosenlundskanalen** (the Paddan Boat terminus), on the right is **Stora Teater**, Scandinavia's only theatre specializing in light opera, ballet and musicals (closed in high summer). Behind it, **Kungsparken** lies along the canal. Opposite the theatre, Trädgårdsföreningen is a favourite park (see p.57). A little further on, to the right off **55**

Avenyn, is the **Röhsska Museet**, which has a notable exhibition of modern design. To the left, housed in the former **Lorensberg Teater**, is the **Museum of Stage History**.

At the south end of Avenyn is **Götaplatsen** – from where, atop its fountain, Carl Milles' statue of **Poseidon** gazes at the world. The square is flanked by Gothenburg's **Stadsteatern** (City Theatre – most events are in Swedish), **Konstmuseet** (Art Museum), **Konserthuset** (Concert Hall, and home to the city's Symphony Orchestra), and the **City Library**.

The **Konstmuseet** has on offer a wonderful collection of Scandinavian paintings, many from the Nordic Light period at the turn of the century, when young artists met at Skagen in north Denmark. This time is portrayed in *Hip, Hip, Hurrah*, PS Krøyer's depiction of the artists toasting one another.

Parks and Excursions

Liseberg, Sweden's biggest and, many would have it, best amusement park, celebrated its 70th anniversary in 1993 with new rides and shows. The park, which is beyond Götaplatsen, first opened on the occasion of the Gothenburg Exhibition in 1923, and has continued to delight visitors ever since.

Poseidon, God of the Sea, as seen by Carl Milles in his statue at Götaplatsen.

Of all Gothenburg's garden parks, **Trädgårdsföreningen** on the banks of Rosenlundskanalen is the most popular. Founded in 1842, and the only one that's acquired a nickname (**Trängår'n**), it has beautiful statues and the **Palmhuset**, a tropical glasshouse from 1878. Another humid place here is **Fjärilshuset**, which is full of tropical butterflies.

Gothenburg's largest park, **Slottskogen** (Castle Wood), offers 137ha (340 acres) of hill, trees and grass, reached from the centre via Linnégata. This is where you'll also find the **Naturhistoriska Museet** (Natural History Museum), which is the country's oldest **Deer Park**, and a children's zoo.

To the south-east, across Dag Hammarskjöldsleden, is Gothenburg's **Botaniska Trädgård** (Botanic Garden), with over 4,000 species in its massive rock garden. On the way to Slottskogen a worthwhile stop is **Feske Kyrka**, a fine fish market that's housed in an old church on the north side of Rosenlundskanalen. It also has a good fish restaurant.

Gothenburg is Sweden's best equipped city for sports, and locals are happiest either sailing in the archipelago or teeing off on one of the area's 24 golf courses. Also here is the **Scandinavium**, one of the largest arenas in Sweden, and the **Åby Trotting Track**.

If you want to take to the water, boats leave from Packhuskajen for **cruises** around the archipelago, with jazz and other bands on board. Shellfish cruises are also offered on the MS *Poseidon*. From Stenpiren, cruises go to the **Vinga Lighthouse** in the islands, or to **Elfsborg Fortress** in the river.

THE COAST

The coasts on either side of Gothenburg are ideal places for bathing and lazing. This whole region is very popular with Swedes, who come to stay in their *stugor* (rustic summer retreats, see p.10).

Bohuslän to the north is an ancient province, as attested by the Bronze Age rock carvings at **Tanum**. The best way to see these figures is on an evening visit organized by the **Vitlycke Hällristningsmuseum** (Rock Carvings Museum), when they can appear to stand out in an almost unearthly way.

North of Strömstad, in an area that has been Norwegian, Danish-Norwegian and then Swedish in turns, the Swedish-Norwegian frontier is marked by a fjord and a high bridge into Norway. Just across the border, at Halden on the Norwegian side, is the remarkable ruin of Frederiksten Fortress, where King Karl XII met his death – an event that brought to an end Sweden's time as a **58** great Baltic power (see p.17).

The small, thinly populated province of Dalsland, north of Bohuslän, has many lakes and is a paradise for boat-lovers. The towns of **Bengtsfors** and **Dals-Ed**, which are really two villages joined by an isthmus with a lake on either side, enjoy some of the nation's most beautiful views. Weaving and winding its way through gentle landscape, the **Dalsland Canal** passes through locks and the awesome **Håverud Aqueduct** as it journeys on its way south to Lake Vänern.

To the south of Gothenburg **Halland** is a family favourite with its seaside towns, among

*A*pron, rubber gloves, base-ball cap – an unlikely uniform for latter-day Swedish fishermen.

them **Kungsbacka**, **Varberg**, **Halmstad**, **Falkenberg** and **Laholm**. (Halmstad has sea routes to Grenå in Denmark.) Inland is rich farming country. East of Kungsbacka, just 26km (18 miles) south of Gothenburg, stands **Fjärås Bräcka** – a great ridge, formed by ancient glaciers, that looks over Lake Lygnern. Here too there are some large Bronze and Iron Age grave fields.

THE LAKES

Sweden's great lakes lie to the north-east of Gothenburg. At 5,650sq km (or 2,180sq miles) **Lake Vänern** is the largest lake in Western Europe, while **Lake Vättern**, at 2,000sq km (750sq miles), is the second largest in Sweden. On the eastern side of Vänern is the Göta Kanal, which links with Lake Vättern *en route* to Stockholm.

In summer these two huge lakes are dotted with boats and swimmers, and the shores with fishermen intent on hooking salmon. Vänern feels like a sea in the middle of Sweden, with Dalsland lying to the west and **Värmland** and **Västergötland** to the north and east. Along the Norwegian border, Värmland is wild and forested.

One of Sweden's most beautiful rivers, Klarälven, flows south to join Vänern at Karlstad and is still used to float logs to the mills. Four-hundred-year-old **Karlstad** was once a trading post and a resting place on the pilgrim route, which followed the Klarälven north to the grave of St Olav the Holy at Trondheim in Norway.

Two other lakeside towns are **Mariestad** to the east, with the towering spire of its 17th-century church and, in the south, **Lidköping**, a porcelain town, which holds a China Festival in August. Between the two is **Kinnekulle**, a beautiful 350m (1,150ft) hill called the 'flowering mountain'.

North of Lidköping on the **Kållandsö Peninsula** is one of **59**

The Göta Canal

Threading its way through the countryside from Gothenburg to Stockholm is the Göta Canal, the first section of which – from Gothenburg to Karlstad on Lake Vänern – opened in 1800.

Today, the Göta Canal is a classic pleasure route, especially popular with Swedes as a trip to mark a decade birthday (much celebrated in Sweden). Routed through the Great Lakes to Mälaren and the west coast, it takes in peaceful countryside and small towns where people turn out to watch the 19th-century canal boats negotiate the locks. *En route* there are sometimes visits to an old *Herrgård* (manor house) for lunch, and all along the way binoculars are out to watch the animals and birds on the banks or on one of the many small islands.

The canal boats run between Stockholm and Gothenburg (and back again) from mid-May to early September. The trip in either direction takes four-five days. Details are available from Rederi AB Göta Canal, Hotellplatsen 2, Box 272, S-401-24 Göteborg; tel. (0) 31-80-63-15.

the finest castles Sweden has to offer, the restored 17th-century **Läckö Slott**.

Great houses dot the areas close to the lakes and Värmland has two in particular. **Rottneros Manor**, on Lake Mellum Fryken, is considered by many the most beautiful in Sweden, while **Mårbacka**, on the other side of the lake, was the home of Swedish writer Selma Lagerlöf (1858-1940), the first woman to be awarded a Nobel prize (1909). Selma Lagerlöf brought fame to this area with books such as *The Story of Gösta Berling*.

On the west shore of Lake Vättern, **Karlsborg** is dominated by a huge 19th-century fortress, including **Slutvärnet** – at 680m (2,230ft) said to be Europe's longest building. At the lake's southernmost point is **Jönköping**, once a market town and now the capital of north Småland (see pp.44-48).

The safety match was invented – and is still made – here, and the old factory is now a museum. To the east is **Huskvarna**, where weapons were made 300 years ago. The smithies are now a craft centre.

North from Jönköping on the lovely lakeside road is the idyllic little town of **Gränna**. This was the birthplace of aviator SA Andrée, who in 1897 tried to cross the North Pole in an air balloon. (His body was later found on White Island in 1930). Each year Gränna celebrates the flight with balloon events, and there are many exhibits in the **Andrée Museet**. While here, try the local specialities of luscious pears and *polkagrisar*, a red and white, peppermint rock, which you can watch being made in one of the *polkagrisar* bakeries.

From Gränna it's just a short boat trip to the narrow isle of **Visingsö**. There, horse-drawn carriages take visitors to the 17th-century **Visingborg Slott**, which held prisoners during Karl XII's wars with Russia.

Further north and, thanks to the Holy Birgitta, on a grander scale, is **Vadstena** with its beautiful 14th-century church. Born in 1303 into the noble Folkung family, Birgitta gave up temporal life at the age of 40 after bringing six children into the world. She moved to Rome, where she founded the St Birgittine Order.

After her death her body was brought back to Vadstena. Ironically, over a century later, Gustav Vasa, the architect of the Swedish Reformation (see p.14), built a great fortress castle nearby. Church and castle still stand there today.

The Central Heartlands

Seven provinces link the south of Sweden to its vast northern stretches, taking in a swathe of countryside and wilderness from the Norwegian border to the Gulf of Bothnia. They are, going from south to north, the coastal provinces of Gästrik-land, Hälsingland, Medelpad and Ångermanland, and the inland provinces of Dalarna, Härjedalen and Jämtland, the last two both great sweeps of forest, river and rising mountains. Even though they are on the eastern side of the country, Medelpad and Ångermanland form the county known, oddly enough, as Västernorrland – or West Norrland!

*T*raditional Dalahäst (horses) are painted red – the colour of many Dalarna houses (right).

DALARNA – THE FOLKLORE PROVINCE

Dalarna is the heart of all things Swedish, where the old traditions and costumes are as natural a part of 'feast' days as they were 100 years ago. **Lake Siljan**, which legend says was gouged out of the landscape by a falling meteor, is the symbol of these folklore traditions.

Indeed, nowhere is the feast of **Midsommar** (Midsummer) celebrated more enthusiastically than in the lakeside communities – where the wooden houses are painted a special dark red with white trimmings. Dancers kick their heels around the decorated Maypole into the summer night, boosting their energy with traditional dishes.

Local people in costume row the long 'church-boats' to **Rättvik Kyrka** at the south-eastern end of the lake, after the times when this was the easiest way to journey in from outlying farms. The 13th-century church has some interesting paintings of Bible characters.

The towns around Siljan are all different. Perched above the lake and affording lovely views, **Tällberg** is one of the most popular holiday spots. **Nusnäs** is the main source of the *Dalahäst* (Dalarna horse), a carved wooden horse painted bright red. During the summer you can watch the carving and painting in the small factory.

At **Mora**, **Zorngården** was the home of **Anders Zorn** (1860-1920), a painter whose lavish works were part of the National Romantic movement of the time. His studio is as he left it. Zorn was the friend of another Dalarna painter, Carl Larsson (see p.64).

Bears at the **Grönklitt Bear Sanctuary** a bit further north roam the natural forest of their large enclosures. Visitors walk along paths to special viewing platforms for a superb view of the bears and the surrounding countryside. The park is also a home to wolves.

Church-boats are still made on **Sollerön** island, and traces of the Vikings are found here in several early graves. Above the lake, the 514m (1,650ft) **Gesundaberget** gives a fine view all round and is home to a southerly **Santaworld**, which offers a mixture of animals, toy workshops and a resident Santa. **Leksand**'s open-air theatre holds annual performances of **Himlaspelet**, a mystery play.

An Industrial Past

The area around Lake Siljan – and particularly around Falun to the south-east – is a paradise for industrial archaeologists, thanks to the industries that sprang up in the wake of mining in the Bergslagen district in the neighbouring province of Västmanland. Forestry and textiles, too, have helped to shape this part of the country, and many successors of the

blast furnaces and giant water-wheels that powered the early mills still continue today, with hi-tech companies now complementing a spectacular industrial history dating from the early 16th century.

The **Stora Kopparberget** (or great copper mine) at Falun is famous. Visitors to the mine don helmet and boots for a long underground tour that can only inspire admiration for the early miners and the feats they achieved in harsh conditions. Stora, the company that owns the mine, is the world's oldest, having been founded in 1288. It is sad that after 800 years of mining, production has recently come to an end.

(Incidentally, the pigment used for the traditional dark red paint that coats most Swedish wooden buildings is a copper-based product.)

Close to Falun, **Sundborn** is the home of the painter Carl Larsson (1853-1919). You can go on guided tours of his house, as well as of **Sundborn Kyrka** and the parsonage, both of which have paintings by the artist on show.

A Selection of Swedish Hotels and Restaurants

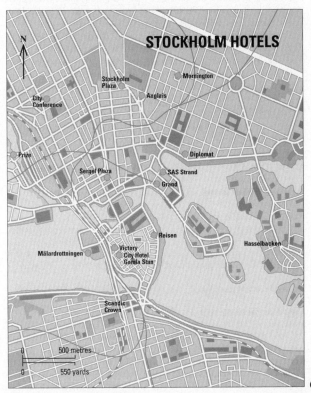

STOCKHOLM HOTELS

N

Mornington

Stockholm Plaza

Anglais

City Conference

Diplomat

Prize

Sergel Plaza

SAS Strand

Grand

Reisen

Hasselbacken

Mälardrottningen

Victory
City Hotel
Gamla Stan

Scandic Crown

0   500 metres

0   550 yards

Recommended Hotels

Sweden has so many hotels in so many places that it is impossible to cover every area in full. Our list gives a selection in the three main cities, plus a few in more widespread areas. In the north in particular, except in towns, hotels may be far apart. In central and north Sweden many hotels and inns also have self-catering *stugor* for 2-6 people in their grounds. Hostel-style accommodation is not uncommon in the wilderness areas.

Hotels are of a high standard, but not cheap. MOMS (VAT) on hotels has, however, been reduced from 25% to 12%.

The price categories below are based on two people sharing a double room at full rates, including substantial cold-table breakfast, MOMS and service charge.

III	Above 1,800 Skr
II	1100-1,800 Skr
I	Below 1,100 Skr

STOCKHOLM

Anglais RESO Hotel II
Humlegårdsgatan 23
S-10220 Stockholm
Tel. (0) 8-614-16-00
Fax (0) 8-611-09-72
Modern hotel opposite Humlegården Park. 212 rooms, plus a number of comfortable cabins for hurried business travellers.

City Conference Hotel II
Wallingatan, S-10724 Stockholm
Tel. (0) 8-20-15-20
Fax (0) 8-791-50-50
Comfortable hotel, recently opened, quiet and well-planned with an outdoor terrace.

City Hotel Gamla Stan I
Lilla Nygatan 25
S-111028 Stockholm
Tel. (0) 8-24-44-50
Fax (0) 8-21-64-83
Occupying a 15th-century building at the Gamla Stan's south end. Unlicensed, popular with business and budget travellers. 51 rooms.

Claes på Hornet II
Surbrunnsgatan 20
S-11248 Stockholm
Tel. (0) 8-16-51-30
Fax (0) 8-612-53-15
Once an 18th-century inn, now a small hotel (10 rooms only) with a lovely atmosphere. Situated in a quiet area, north of the centre.

Grand Hotel   III

S Blasieholmen 8
S-10383 Stockholm
Tel. (0) 8-679-35-00
Fax (0) 8-611-86-86
Luxury hotel overlooking water to
Gamla Stan and the Royal Palace.
Excellent restaurants. 321 rooms.

Hasselbacken Hotel   II

Hazeliusbacken 20
S-10055 Stockholm
Tel. (0) 8-670-50-50
Fax (0) 8-663-84-10
Mansion-style building grafted on
to 19th-century timber restaurant.
Views over Djurgården Royal Park.
Handy for museums, Skansen and
Gröna Lund. 112 rooms.

Hotell Diplomat   I

Strandvägen 7C
S-10440 Stockholm
Tel. (0) 8-663-58-00
Fax (0) 8-783-66-34
Fine waterfront hotel built in 1911
in *Jugend* style. Looks towards the
boats at Nybroviken. 133 rooms.

Hotell Mälardrottningen II

Riddarholmen
S-11128 Stockholm
Tel. (0) 8-24-36-00
Fax (0) 8-24-36-76
One of Stockholm's most unusual
places to stay: boat hotel in 1920s
luxury yacht formerly owned by

American millionairess Barbara
Hutton. Situated in lovely anchor-
age at Riddarholmen. Cabins are
now hotel rooms. Gourmet restaurant (see p.79). 59 rooms.

Källhagens Wärdshus   II

Djurgårdbrunnsvägen 10
S-115267 Stockholm
Tel. (0) 8-667-60-60
Fax (0) 8-667-60-43
Classic modern building (1990) in
the style of a traditional 18th-cen-
tury 'Red House', in idyllic setting
2km (1½ miles) from city centre
on Djurgårdsdviken (bay). Famed
for its food.

Långholmen   I

Gamla Kronohäktet
S-10072 Stockholm
Tel. (0) 8-668-05-00
Fax (0) 84-10-96
Unusual hotel in a former prison.
Located on island but convenient
for the centre by car or by public
transport. Also offers Youth Hos-
tel accommodation. 101 rooms.

Mornington Hotel   II

Nybrogatan 53
S-10244 Stockholm
Tel. (0) 8-663-12-40
Fax (0) 8-662-21-79
Central hotel, close to museums.
English-style lobby bar and res-
taurant. 140 rooms.

67

Prize Hotel I

Kungsbron 1
S-11122 Stockholm
Tel.(0) 8-14-94-50
Fax (0) 8-14-98-48
Next door to World Trade Centre, modern building (1989) with lots of glass. Breakfast hotel, popular with business travellers, but also a good family hotel. 158 rooms.

Reisen RESO Hotel III

Skeppsbron 12-14
S-11130 Stockholm
Tel. (0) 8-22-32-60
Fax (0) 8-20-15-59
Well-known 19th-century hotel on waterfront in Gamla Stan, with fine view towards Saltsjön. Good sauna. Piano bar. 114 rooms.

SAS Strand Hotel II

Nybrokajen 9
Box 16396, S-10327 Stockholm
Tel. (0) 8-678-78-00
Fax (0) 8-611-24-36
Traditional building overlooking boats, with good view from its bar and restaurant on the top floor.

Scandic Crown Hotel II

Guldgrånd 8
Box 15270, S-10465 Stockholm
Tel. (0) 8-702-25-00
Fax (0) 8-642-83-58
Above Slussen, overlooks Gamla Stan, Lake Mälaren and Saltsjön.

Known for its restaurant, exclusive wine cellar and original spirit shop from 1700. 319 rooms.

Sergel Plaza RESO II
Hotel

Brunkebergstorg 9
Box 16411, S-10327 Stockholm
Tel. (0) 8-22-66-00
Fax (0) 8-21-50-70
On peaceful square set back from Hamngatan, in centre of Stockholm. Comfortable lobby café and piano bar, and a good international restaurant. 406 rooms.

Stockholm Plaza II

Birger Jarlsgatan 29
S-10328 Stockholm
Tel. (0) 8-14-51-20
Fax (0) 8-210-34-92
Unusual, stone-built 19th-century hotel with a pleasant atmosphere. Surrounded by shops and outdoor cafés, handy for centre and close to Humlegård Park. 151 rooms.

Victory Hotel III

Lilla Nygatan 5
S-11128 Stockholm
Tel. (0) 8-14-30-90
Fax (0) 8-20-21-77
17th-century building on a quiet street, close to Mälaren. Famous for its Lord Nelson memorabilia. Remains of the medieval city wall visible. 48 rooms.

STOCKHOLM'S SURROUNDINGS

Grand Hotel Saltsjöbaden

S-13983 Saltsjöbaden
Tel. (0) 8-717-00-20
Fax (0) 8-717-95-31
Castle-style hotel set on the edge of Baggensfjärden. Good service, and food. Swimming, sailing, tennis, fishing and golf facilities available. 105 rooms.

Gripsholms Värdshus and Hotel

Kyrkogatan 1
S-64700 Mariefred
Tel. (0)159-130-20
Fax (0)159-109-74
In close proximity to Mälaren and the boat landing stage, with a good view of Gripsholm Slott. Sauna, gym, billiards and marked walking paths. 45 rooms.

Hotell Linné

Skolgatan 45
S-75002, Uppsala
Tel. (0)18-10-20-00
Fax (0)18-761-74
Excellent location in the heart of Uppsala but next to Linnétrtädgården (Linné Gardens – the great botanist's legacy to his university town – see p.34). Fine restaurant. Closed July. 117 rooms.

Hotell Svava

Bangården 24, Box 1425
S-75144 Uppsala
Tel. (0)18-13-00-30
Fax (0)18-13-22-30
New hotel, centrally situated and close to most sights. Well-equipped rooms plus an indoor shopping complex. 111 rooms.

Kohlswa Herrgård

S-73030 Kolsva, near Arboga
Tel. (0)221-509-00
Fax (0)221-511-80
25km (16 miles) north of Arboga surrounded by its own parkland. Riding, fishing, shooting, tennis, golf, and walking. 44 rooms.

Sigtunastiftelsens Gästhem

Manfred Björkquists allé 2-4
S-19322 Sigtuna
Tel. (0) 8-592-589-00
Fax (0) 8-592-589-99
Located in woods near Mälaren. Cloister-like building with beautiful rose garden. 51 rooms.

Waxholms Hotell

Hamngatan 2
Box 63, S-18521 Vaxholm
Tel. (0) 8-541-301-50
Fax (0) 8-541-313-76
Comfortable, modest hotel set on Vaxholm island – ideal for watersports. 32 rooms.

69

MALMÖ

Garden Hotel

Baltzarsgatan 20, Box 4075
S-20311 Malmö
Tel. (0) 40-10-40-00
Fax (0) 40-11-68-08
Quiet, comfortable hotel with a beautiful lobby-loung. Central location. 172 rooms.

Hotell Kramer

Stortorget 7
S-20121 Malmö
Tel. (0) 40-701-20
Fax (0) 40-12-69-41
Classic, turreted white building in Malmö's old main square. Good dining, nightclub. 45 rooms.

SAS Royal

Östergatan 10
S-21125 Malmö
Tel. (0) 40-23-92-00
Fax (0) 40-11-28-40
Half-timbered house with comfortable rooms. Restaurant claims best steak in Malmö. 221 rooms.

Scandic Crown Hotel

Amiralsgatan 19
S-21127 Malmö
Tel. (0) 40-10-07-30
Fax (0) 40-11-92-24
Modern hotel with a lot of glass in the concert-hall building. Popular nightclub, health club. 154 rooms.

THE SOUTH

Halltorps Gästgiveri

Högsrum,
S-38792 Borgholm, Öland
Tel (0) 485-850-00
Fax (0) 485-850-01
17th-century inn, 9km (6 miles) from Borgholm on Öland. Superb restaurant. Swimming, riding, golf and bird-watching. 36 rooms.

Karlelby Kro

S-27293 Tommarp, Skåne
Tel. (0) 414-203-00
Fax (0) 414-204-73
Charming, white farmhouse 7km (4 miles) west of Simrishamn, with a gourmet menu and fine wines. Pool, sauna and gym. 21 rooms.

Örenäs Slott

S-26163 Glumslöv, Landskrona
Tel. (0) 418-702-30
Fax (0) 418-731-81
Stately building in splendid park overlooking Öresund strait. Tennis and swimming. 128 rooms.

Slottshotellet – Romantik Hotel

Slottsvägen 7, S-39233 Kalmar
Tel. (0) 480-882-60
Fax (0) 480-119-93
View over Kalmarsund, and almost next to castle. Restaurant, bar, sauna and solarium. 36 rooms.

Star Hotel Lund ▐▐

Glimmervågen 5, Box 110-26
S-22011 Lund
Tel. (0) 46-11-20-00
Fax (0) 46-11-50-00
Seven minutes' walk from the city centre. Sauna, pool and solarium, and close to golf, tennis and badminton facilities, as well as a jogging track. 196 rooms.

Strand Hotel ▐▐

Strandgatan 34
S-62156 Visby, Gotland
Tel. (0) 498-21-26-00
Fax (0) 498-27-81-11
Modern hotel in the heart of old Visby on Gotland island. Close to the shore and old city walls, as well as clematis house and botanic gardens. Sauna and small indoor pool. 110 rooms.

GOTHENBURG

Hotell Eggers ▐▐

Drottningtorget
S-40125 Göteborg
Tel. (0) 31-80-60-70
Fax (0) 31-15-42-43
Classic railway hotel, with marble floors, pillars, great chandeliers and plants all helping to confirm that it is Gothenburg's oldest, built in the mid-19th century. Close to Central Station, airport terminus and Nordstan shopping. 88 rooms.

Hotell Ekoxen ▐▐

Norra Hamngatan 38
S-41106 Göteborg
Tel. (0) 31-80-50-80
Fax (0) 31-15-33-70
Small Best Western hotel in a fine 1850 building, at Nordstan centre, close to Gustav Adolfs Torg. Free herring buffet for guests. 74 rooms.

Hotell Liseberg Heden ▐▐

Sten Sturegatan
S-41138 Göteborg
Tel. (0) 31-20-02-80
Fax (0) 31-16-52-83
Set in Heden (heath). Pretty buildings in traditional style. Free ticket to nearby Amusement Park included. Good for families. 159 rooms.

Hotell Onyxen ▐

Sten Sturegatan 23
S-41253 Göteborg
Tel. (0) 31-81-08-45
Fax (0) 31-16-56-72
Attractive, small breakfast hotel, in elegant, turn-of-the-century, six-storey house. Family-owned. Opposite Scandinavium. 34 rooms.

Hotell Riverton ▐▐▐

Stora Badhusgatan 26
S-41121 Göteborg
Tel. (0) 31-10-12-00
Fax (0) 31-13-08-66
Close to north harbour and site of the new Opera House, and offer- **71**

ing wonderful view of estuary from 11th-storey Sky Bar and Restaurant. Family-owned. 190 rooms.

RESO Hotel Rubinen   IIII
Kungsportavenyn 24
S-40014 Göteborg
Tel. (0) 31-81-08-00
Fax (0) 31-16-75-86
Occupies an excellent position on Avenyn, with the popular Restaurant Andra Våningen (see p.79) and Bistro. 185 rooms.

Scandic Crown   IIII
Polhemsplatsen 3
S-41111 Göteborg
Tel. (0) 31-80-09-00
Fax (0) 31-15-45-88
Modern hotel with lovely atrium restaurant. Sauna, solarium, gym and pool bar. Family rooms available for two adults, two children. Close to Central Station and airport bus terminal. 320 rooms.

Spar Hotel   I
Karl Johansgatan 66-70
S-41455 Göteborg
Tel. (0) 31-42-00-20
Fax (0) 31-42-63-83
Cosy breakfast hotel near the old Majorna harbour, now a shopping area. Trams to the centre, and there is a *Systembolaget* (alcohol shop) next door! Good rooms at budget price. 150 rooms.

THE WEST

Fregattan Home Hotel   II
Hamnplan, S-43244 Varberg
Tel. (0) 340-770-00
Fax (0) 340-111-21
In harbour square, with fine view of boats. Virtually on the bathing beach. Close to ferry to Grenå in Denmark. Closed July. 98 rooms.

Hotell Alphyddan   I
Långatan 6, S-44030 Marstrand
Tel. (0) 303-610-30/38
Fax (0)303-612-00
A few yards from a swimming pool and the famous little harbour, in a town without cars, the gateway to Bohuslän's southern archipelago. Well known for its cellar. 35 rooms.

Hotell Carl XII   I
Storgatan 41, S-66800 Dals-Ed
Tel. (0) 634-111-55
Fax (0) 534-122-24
Beautifully situated old hotel between two lakes, but close to centre of village. Bicycles and canoes for hire, sauna and billiards. 38 rooms, plus hostel accommodation.

Ronnums Herrgård   I
S-46830 Vargön, near Vänersborg
Tel. (0) 521-22-32-70
Fax (0)521-22-06-60
Superb *Relais et Châteaux* manor house in parkland south of Lake

Vänern. Celebrated for its gourmet food, informality and good service. Golf, tennis, watersports and elk safaris arranged. 61 rooms.

Sunds Herrgård

S-56028 Lekeryd
near Jönköping
Tel. (0) 36-820-06
Fax (0) 36-821-40
Country house hotel on Lake Nåtarn. Good food and all comforts. Wildlife park, boating, fishing, riding, walking and swimming. 80 rooms (including chalets).

Tanums Gestgifveri

S-45700 Tanumshede
Tel. (0) 525-290-10
Fax (0) 525-295-71
Charming 17th-century inn, well known for gourmet cuisine. Situated close to the famous prehistoric carvings and many beautiful fishing villages. Golf, tennis and fishing available. 29 rooms.

Vadstena Klosterhotel

Klosterområdet, S-59230 Vadstena
Tel. (0) 143-115-30/130-00
Fax (0) 143-136-48
One of Sweden's oldest hotels in a 12th-century building. Next door to Skt Birgitta Kyrka on Lake Vättern, and five minutes' from Gustav Vasa's castle. Many original features. Restaurant. 29 rooms.

Värdshuset Hvitan

Storgatan 24
S-31121 Falkenberg
Tel. (0) 346-820-90
Fax (0) 346-597-96
A lovely 18th-century listed building in Falkenberg's old centre, with a garden leading down to the river. Close to sandy beaches. Golf and salmon fishing almost on the doorstep! Sea sports. 35 rooms.

THE CENTRAL HEARTLAND

Fryksås Hotell

S-79498 Orsa
Tel. (0) 250-460-20
Fax (0) 250-460-90
Situated on high southern slopes above lakes Siljan and Orsasjön, with fine views over surrounding countryside. Within walking distance of Grönklitt Bear Park and a ski resort. Gourmet food and a strong musical tradition. Golf, tennis, fishing and skiing. 13 rooms.

Green Hotel

S-79370 Tällberg
Tel. (0) 247-502-50
Fax (0) 247-501-30
Rooms at different prices in various buildings with views of Lake Siljan, the oldest dating from the 16th century and housing many antiques and works of art. Waiters **73**

wear local costume. Both indoor and outdoor swimming pools.

Hotell Diplomatt

S-83013 Åre
Tel. (0) 647-502-65
Fax (0) 647-507-53
Set in a charming turn-of-the-century hotel and ski lodge right in the centre of Åre. Sauna and good après-ski, as well as a restaurant and a disco. 170 rooms plus 280 in the ski lodge.

Hotell Södra Berget

Södra Stadsberget, Box 858
S-85124 Sundsvall
Tel. (0) 60-12-30-00
Fax (0) 60-15-10-34
Wonderful position at the top of Södra Berget, one of Sundsvall's two outlook hills, 3km (2 miles) from the centre. Fabulous views, sauna, fitness room, slalom run, walking and skiing. 181 rooms.

Hotel Tänndalen

S-84098 Tänndalen
Tel. (0) 684-220-20
Fax (0) 684-224-24
Family-run establishment situated in a popular all-year mountain resort area. Excellent food, wonderful mountain panorama, and indoor pool, golf, fishing, shooting and canoeing available. Miles of ski tracks close by. 66 rooms.

Järvsöbaden Hotell

S-82040 Järvsö
Tel. (0) 651-404-01
Fax (0) 651-417-37
Rural hotel owned and run by the same family since it was built at the turn of the century. Situated on Öjeberget mountain, close to Järvsö Zoo on the outskirts of town. The grounds are lovely, and you can enjoy the tennis court, pool, fishing and riding. 45 rooms.

Mjälloms Hotell

Hotellgatan 3
S-87031 Mjällom
Tel. (0) 613-211-14
Fax (0) 613-214-75
Occupies fantastic position on a point between two bays. Swimming (2km/1 mile to the beach), walking and jogging, fishing, golf and a marina. Smörgåsbord with local specialities. 16 rooms.

RESO Hotel Örnsköldsvik

Lasarettsgatan 2, Box 10
S-891121 Örnsköldsvik
Tel. (0) 660-101-10
Fax (0) 660-837-91
Standard RESO hotel close to the centre and station and only a short walk away from the harbour, sea and new 'Paradisbadet' (fun pools). Restaurant, bar and brasserie on the spot. 115 rooms.

RESO Hotel Sundsvall ▐▐

Esplanaden 29
S-85232 Sundsvall
Tel. (0) 60-17-16-00
Fax (0) 60-12-20-30

Modern hotel in big red building, centrally located. Leisure centre with solarium, sauna, pool, jacuzzi and bar. Restaurant, disco, piano bar and casino. 203 rooms.

RESO Hotel Winn ▐▐

Prästgatan 16
S-83131 Östersund
Tel. (0) 63-12-77-40
Fax (0) 63-10-67-29

Good RESO hotel in a central position on Stortorget, and with a restaurant, cocktail bar, pool and sauna. 177 rooms.

Scandic Hotel ▐

Montörsbacken 4
S-82600 Söderhamn
Tel. (0) 270-180-20
Fax (0) 270-189-01

Well-furnished hotel with modern facilities. Restaurant and taverna-style fare. 87 rooms.

Ulfshyttans Herrgård ▐

S-78196 Borlänge
Tel. (0) 243-513-00
Fax (0) 243-511-11

Old manor house with unusual turret rooms and a restaurant over-looking Lake Ulfssjön, as well as a library of old books and an art gallery. In the grounds there is a ruined 18th-century blast-furnace (a reminder of Bergeslagen's iron-smelting days). 20 rooms.

Åkerblads Hotell Gästgiveri ▐

S-79303 Tällberg
Tel. (0) 247-508-00
Fax (0) 247-502-00

The Akerblad family have owned this building ever since the 16th century (when it was a traveller's resting place). It only became a hotel earlier this century, and is still run by the Akerblads. All built in solid timber with an old log cabin. Traditional bar, good home cooking. 89 rooms.

NORRLAND AND THE ARCTIC

Hotel Jokkmokk ▐▐

Solgatan 45
S-96040 Jokkmokk
Tel. (0) 971-113-20
Fax (0) 971-116-25

A good hotel in the heart of Sami country, with a restaurant that serves local specialities. Cocktail bar. The area offers many activities, including helicopter transport to national parks, scooter safaris, fishing instruction and competitions. 75 rooms.

Hotell Laponia

Storgatan 45
S-93300 Arvidsjaur
Tel. (0) 960-108-80
Fax (0) 960-104-89
Comfortable, cosy, modern hotel, close to Arvidsjaur's main lake. The restaurant serves Norrland specialities. There is a popular pub and disco and the hotel is a good base for rafting, walking, climbing and skiing. 115 rooms.

Hotell Nordkalotten

Lulviksvägen 1, S-95162 Luleå
Tel. (0) 920-893-50
Fax (0) 920-199-09
Beautiful position on the heath, beside a small lake with cabins dotted among 800-year-old pines. Well located for outdoor activities: walking, cross-country skiing and swimming. Indoor pool, sauna and solarium; free loan of sports gear. 171 rooms.

Hotell Toppen

Blåvägen 238, S-92300 Storuman
Tel. (0) 951-117-00
Fax (0) 951-121-57
Situated in a pine wood and handy for mountain walking and skiing, but also very close to the railway station. Restaurant, pub, fishing as well as a panoramic sauna with views over Storumansjön lake and mountain scenery. 63 rooms.

Jukkasjärvi Wärdshus and Hembygdsgård

Jukkasjärvi S-98191
Tel. (0) 980-211-09
Fax (0) 980-214-06
Get close to nature beside Torneälven river in a well-restored old timber building which is now an inn, 25km (18 miles) from Kiruna. Hotel-standard *stugor* (cabins) plus more basic accommodation, and local food. Good for outdoor activities: rafting, fishing, riding and dog sledging. 45 four-bed *stugor*. (Runs the Arctic Hallen or ice hall from January to May, see p.96.)

Lövånger Kyrkby

Lövånger
Tel. (0) 913-103-95
Fax (0) 913-107-59
For a change, try this restored church village from the 15th century. Beautifully refurbished cottages, restaurant, leisure room and sauna. 77 rooms.

Motell Björnen

Björnvägen 3, S-90640 Umeå
Tel. (0) 90-13-71-10
Fax (0) 90-11-74-11
Situated close to woodlands, 3km (2 miles) from the centre and 1km (½ mile) from the ski lift, with sauna, floodlit tracks, bathing and fishing in Nydalssjön lake. 40 rooms.

Nya Dundret

Box 812, S-98221 Gällivare
Tel. (0) 970-145-60
Fax (0) 970-148-27
Set on a lower plateau of Dundret, some 4km (3 miles) from the station, with rooms, suites and 90 *stugor* (cabins). Good base for skiing, fishing, and guided walking tours. 125 rooms.

Prize Hotel

Rådhusplatsen 14, S-90328 Umeå
Tel. (0) 90-13-23-00
Fax (0) 90-14-23-66
Very central, modern hotel, with well-equipped rooms and facilities. Restaurant, cocktail and piano bars, grill, casino, sauna and fitness room. 165 rooms.

RESO Hotel Ferrum

Lars Janssongatan 15, Box 22
S-98131 Kiruna
Tel. (0) 980-186-00
Fax (0) 980-145-05
Big, modern hotel near the station. Leisure centre, restaurant, cocktail bar and casino. 170 rooms.

SAS Luleå

Storgatan 17, Box 267
S-95131 Luleå
Tel. (0) 920-940-00
Fax (0) 920-882-22
Central hotel, with modern rooms and indoor swimming pool, sauna and health club. Restaurant, night club and wine cellar. 198 rooms.

Silverhatten Hotell

Box 94, S-93090 Arjeplog
Tel. (0) 961-107-70
Fax (0) 961-114-26
Sitting on a mountain above town, with endless views. The restaurant combines good food (game, reindeer) with a panorama. 85 rooms.

STF Mountain Hotel Abisko

S-98024 Abisko
Tel. (0) 980-401-00
Fax (0) 980-401-40
A community in itself in Abisko National Park, close to where the train stops. Apart from the hotel, there are *stugor* (cabins) and hostel accommodation, a provisions shop (and a restaurant and bar in the hotel). Activities include boating, skiing, walking, mountain biking, guides and special guided 'theme' weeks. 195 rooms.

Strand Hotel

Pite Havsbad, S-94128 Piteå
Tel. (0) 911-322-00
Fax (0) 911-323-26
Well-equipped rooms close to the harbour and bathing area, but 10km (7 miles) from the centre. Swimming pool, sea fishing, boats for hire and entertainment. 201 rooms. **77**

Recommended Restaurants

Sweden offers a good range of restaurants in the main cities, but fewer in rural areas, where many of the best are in hotels (see hotel listings on pp.66-77). Portions are generous and salad is often included. On a tight budget, however, make lunch, *dagens rätt* (see p.112), the main meal and look out for offers such as Sunday specials. Tourist information publications such as *Stockholm This Week* give listings. Remember that some restaurants may be closed during July.

Eating out in Sweden can be expensive; one reason is that the bill usually includes 21% MOMS (VAT) and service charge. It is customary to round up the bill to the nearest 10 Skr.

The establishments listed below offer both quality food and service, and represent good value for money. Prices are for an evening meal per person, without wine.

▯▯▯	above (sometimes well above) 250 Skr
▯▯	100-250 Skr
▯	below 100 Skr

STOCKHOLM

Blå Porten Café ▯
Djurgårdsvägen 60
Tel. (0) 8-663-87-59/8-662-71-62
Attractive restaurant in former art gallery, with central garden. Good, simple food, with emphasis on Swedish cuisine.

Centralens Restaurang ▯▯
Central Station
Tel. (0) 8-20-20-9
Set directly above the station hall, this restaurant offers good food, and is especially popular for breakfast. Simple dishes.

Hasselbacken ▯▯▯
Hazeliusbacken 20
Tel. (0) 8-670-50-00
Famous 19th-century restaurant, with the added benefit of a large terrace garden. International and traditional Swedish food served in a beautiful setting.

Hermans, The New Green Kitchen ▯
Stora Nygatan 11
Tel. (0) 8-11-95-00
Highly popular international vegetarian cooking. Its success has spawned a series of other locations throughout the city.

Leijontornet (Victory Hotel)

Lilla Nygatan 5
Tel. (0) 14-23-55
For high-class, traditional Swedish cuisine in historic setting, with a glass floor over the ruins of medieval walls. (Closed July).

Mälardrottningen

Riddarholmen
Tel. (0) 8-24-36-00
International and Swedish cuisine on Barbara Hutton's luxury yacht.

Operakällaren

Operahuset
Tel. (0) 8-676-58-00
A venerable institution (some 200 years old) with fine décor. Haute cuisine and home cooking. Famous for its smörgåsbord.

Stekhuset Falstaff

Tegelundsvägen 90
Tel. (0) 8-63-48-40
Watch your steak being grilled in the open kitchen at this excellent steakhouse.

Victoria

Kungsträdgården
Tel. (0) 8-10-10-85
Good traditional Swedish food overlooking Stockholm's popular garden square, with an outdoor verandah. Open late.

GOTHENBURG

Andra Vånigen

Hotell Rubinen,
Kungsportsavenyn 24
Tel. (0) 31-81-08-80
Chef Christer Svantesson provides gourmet food in his restaurant overlooking Avenyn.

Brassserie Ferdinand

Drottninggatan 41
Tel. (0) 31-10-71-60
A cellar restaurant serving good Swedish country cooking, at reasonable prices.

Gamle Port

Östra Larmgatan 18
Tel. (0) 31-13-10-70
Good international and Swedish food in 19th-century atmosphere.

The Place

Arkivgatan 7
Tel. (0) 31-18-15-66
Gourmet restaurant serving international cuisine in a small street close to Avenyn.

Restaurang Räkan

Loprensbergsgatan 16
Tel. (0) 31-16-98-99
Food and fun! Order shrimps and steer them across the 'pool' in a miniature radio-controlled fishing boat! Will delight children.

Restaurang Wärdshuset ||

Liseberg (0) 31-83-62-77
One of Liseberg's many and varied restaurants, serving good food in a 19th-century atmosphere. Also a café and pub. Summer only.

Sjömagasinet ||

Klippan 6
Tel. (0) 31-24-65-10
Seafood and Swedish specialities restaurant in an historic harbour warehouse built in 1775. Summer only (from 1 April).

MALMÖ

Centralens Restaurant |

Central Station
Tel. (0) 40-766-80
Station restaurant, sometimes with a troubadour in the evening. Snack bar and 'dish of the day'.

Kockska Krogen |||

Stortorget
Tel. (0) 40-730-20
High-class Swedish and international cooking in a vaulted 16th-century building.

Olgas ||

Pildammsparken
Tel. (0) 40-12-55-26
Old inn set in Sweden's largest park. Simple, Swedish-style food.

Rådhuskällaren ||

('Wein und Bierkeller')
Kyrkogatan 6
Tel. (0) 40-790-20
A 16th-century cellar restaurant, specializing in fish.

Restaurant Johan P ||

Saluhallen, Lilla Torg
Tel. (0) 40-97-18-18
Set in Malmö's market hall, specializing in delicious fresh fish.

Restaurant Mongolian Barbecue ||

Södra Promenaden 23
Tel. (0) 46-14-15-16
Meats spiced with sauces together with vegetables, cooked Mongolian style. Waiters are in costume.

Restaurant WB (Wein und Bierkeller) |

Stortorget. Entrance: Kompanigatan
Tel. (0) 46-790-20
Simple, mostly home cooking, such as *pyttipanna* (fried chopped meat, onion and potato with beetroot, gherkin and egg).

Översten ||||

Kronprinsen, Regimentsgatan 52
Tel. (0) 40-91-91-00
Fine international cuisine and the city's best views from the 26th floor, across to Denmark.

COAST AND COUNTRYSIDE

Life in tiny (in Swedish terms) Gästrikland centres on its main town, **Gävle**. Here you'll find a **Railway Museum**, including an 1874 coach of the veteran traveller, King Oscar II.

The main coast road, the E4, sets out across Sweden's immense distances, passing Söderhamn and Hudiksvall – Hälsingland's two principal coastal towns – Sundsvall and Härnösand on the Medelpad-Ångermanland border, as well as **Örnsköldsvik**, 700km (435 miles) north of Stockholm.

Up the coast are many small fishing villages, where Baltic herring comes into its own – served with dill or sometimes smoked golden brown and called *böckling*. Not far north of Gävle, herring from **Bonan** is particularly famous (and is usually smelt before it's seen).

Söderhamn goes back to the 17th century, when it was built as an army town (the armoury is now a museum). To the west, **Bollnäs** has since 1919 been the home of a favourite Swe-

dish sweet, a peppermint once boiled in a house kitchen. Today you can still see it being boiled in this traditional way.

Dalarna may be known as the 'folklore province', but it is Hälsingland that plays host to the **Hälsingehambo**, Sweden's biggest folk-dancing competition. On an early June morning in the Ljusnån valley, north of Bollnäs, the fiddles strike up *Hårgalåten* and 3,000 people begin dancing up the valley towards **Järvsö**. They dance in several stages (with bus rides in between) from 6am until 10pm! Along the route you'll find scores of dancers at the roadside taking off their shoes to wriggle their toes in relief. The 'Hambo' ends happily with the best 100 couples dancing in a final competition at Stenegård, Järvsö's manor house.

Delsbo, further north, rivals the Hambo with a fiddlers' rally in early July. Hundreds of fiddlers gather at the **Delsbostämman** folk festival.

The old, prosperous iron-masters of this area left their legacy in many places, including the **Galtström Bruk** (or **81** ironworks) on the Ljungån to the west of Sundsvall. Built in 1673 and closed in 1917, the whole site, from blast furnace and foundry to elegant manor house and workers' dwellings, is in excellent condition.

In the same valley, on the E14 from Sundsvall and Ånge, **Flataklocken** rises to 465m (1,500ft). It is the true centre of Sweden, with a road to the top, an observation tower and a panorama that stretches for miles. You can get a certificate to prove you have been there in the village of Munksbysjön, near the foot of the hill.

Sundsvall, on the Gulf of Bothnia, is largely stone, risen from the ashes of the Great Fire of 1888, which destroyed half the town. It was rebuilt in style by the timber barons.

Several northern towns on the Gulf of Bothnia suffered in Swedish-Russian conflicts. After **Härnösand** was raided in 1721, few of the early buildings were left apart from the wooden houses in **Östanbäcken**. The best view of town and harbour is from **Murberget** open-air museum, second only to Stockholm's magnificent Skansen (see p.31).

The Legend of the Hälsingehambo

This feat of long-distance dancing has its origins in a weird and macabre legend from long ago. One day, so the story goes, a strange fiddler arrived to lead the villagers in their celebratory dance. No one knew him, but he played well and the dancers followed, little realizing that this was no human fiddler, but the Devil himself.

All day the dancing continued as the fiddler urged on their tired bodies with alluring tunes. When daylight faded, still they followed him up the exhausting route up Hårgaberget, a local mountain. At the summit they danced on, spinning around in a circle that never broke. As daylight returned, however, all that remained was their skulls, whirling forever to form a ring that – it is said – you can still find shining white in the mountain rock.

Just north of Härnösand is a memorial to the strikers shot by soldiers during the Hungry Thirties (see p.20). The statue – by sculptor Lenny Clarhäll – was erected in 1981 at Lunde, right at the southern end of the beautiful Sandöbro bridge.

Kramfors, 10km (6 miles) further north and on the same side of the river, is Sweden's accordionists' town, thanks to musician Kalle Grönstedt. It is also the home town of Frans Berwald (1796-1868), one of the first Swedish composers. Berwald was a violinist and infant prodigy who played in Stockholm's Court Chapel when still a child.

Härnosand is the start of a little-known part of this coast that is too good to miss, the beautiful **Höga Kusten** (High Coast), stretching 80km (56 miles) north to Örnsköldsvik, with the **Nordingrå peninsula** as its centre.

The High Coast may have remained a secret because it is hard to see from the E4. The simplest detour is to turn right off the road at Gallsäter into a world of high cliffs, inlets, bays and islands. There are tiny villages, wonderful places to swim and little restaurants where you can get a taste of *husmanskost* (home cooking).

At the northern end of the High Coast is **Varvsberget**, which rises out of the town of Örnsköldsvik (also known as Övik). The mountain is a good place for a view over the Gulf of Bothnia and nearby islands, home to the fishermen-farmers of old. Most of that way of life has gone from the islands, but from Övik it is still possible to see some genuine fishing villages on Ulvön and Trysunda, which have some lovely old fishing chapels.

FOREST, MOUNTAIN AND RIVER

Where the great rivers rise in the mountains of Härjedalen and Jämtland, close to the Norwegian border, you will come across some magnificent waterfalls. **Tännforsen**, west of Östersund, is the most famous in Sweden, with a drop of 30m (100ft) in a massive white wall that later becomes Indalsälven. **83**

Further north, **Hällingsåfallet** has over thousands of years bitten and scraped into the surrounding rock face to form Europe's largest filled canyon. There is the thrill of white-water rafting on many of these rivers, as well as canoeing and some superb fishing.

The slopes of Härjedalen and Jämtland offer facilities for skiing, walking and climbing, as well as mountain-biking and pony-trekking. The forests are carpeted with delicate flowers

In Jämtland, snow means skiing and après-ski at resorts like Åre, **84** *below Åreskutan's great heights.*

and abundant wild berries such as raspberries, blueberries and *hjortron* (cloudberries) – all favourites in the great Swedish pastime of berry-picking.

This is the land where the elk is king. A bull, weighing up to 500kg, is a magnificent sight, but you will have to move very quietly to get close. The most likely view is from a car ('Beware of Elks' is a familiar road sign), for the elks sometimes come down to the roadside at sunset or sunrise.

A variety of other animals might be seen, including otters and beavers – and, well hidden in the remoter areas, lynx and wolverines. Bird watchers may catch sight of ravens, eagles and some unusual species of owl. **Sånfjället National Park**, which lies on the south side of Highway 84 in Härjedalen (north-west of Sveg), contains the largest population of wild bears in the country and runs expeditions to see them.

Härjedalen is the highest province in Sweden, with the highest village, **Tännäs**, and the highest A-road (84), which runs over the **Flatruet Plateau**.

From here you can get a good view of Sweden's most southerly glacier on **Helagsfjället**, just east of the Norwegian border. At 1,796m (6,000ft), this is the highest peak south of the Arctic Circle.

The way into these wild, isolated spots is from the south on Highway 45 or east-west from Hudiksvall on Highway 84, following the course of the River Ljusnån. The two highways intersect at **Sveg**, Härjedalen's main town. Sveg's open-air museum, **Gammelgården**, has 20 old buildings. The **King's Stone**, erected in 1909, marks the arrival of the railway in the town, while the railway bridge over the quiet waters of the Ljusnån is truly a masterpiece of engineering. A relaxing way to travel into Härjedalen and Jämtland is by rail, with good links from the south. For railway connoisseurs, the scenic *Inlandsbanan* line (see p.91) heads north from Östersund.

Lake Storsjön is to this area what Lake Siljan is to Dalarna. Sweden's fifth largest lake, it lies right in the centre of the two provinces, with the old island of **Frösön** linked by a bridge to the main town of **Östersund**, which was founded by Gustav III in 1786.

Frösön is named after Frö or Frej, the goddess of fertility, from the long-ago days when the islanders worshipped the Norse Gods. At the Frösön end of the bridge you will find the country's northernmost rune stone, which is 1,000 years old.

Frösö Kyrka, built over a sacrificial grove of the ancient Æsur religion, is very popular for weddings. Every summer Frösön is the venue for performances of the well-known Viking story *Arnljot*, turned into an opera (one of five) by the composer Wilhelm Peterson-Berger (1867-1942), who lived here. Frösön also boasts a **Zoo and Tropical House** with over 500 animals. A trip to the top of **Frösö Tornet**, some 468m (1,560ft) high, will reward the climber with superb views.

The oldest coal-fired steam-ship still in use in Sweden, the **SS Thomée**, plies the lake, the depths of which are said to conceal a creature along the lines of Scotland's Loch Ness monster. Many sightings have been claimed, but its existence has not been confirmed so far. For the curious, there is a dis-play of monster-catching gear in the **Länsmuseet**. The beast itself is described as 'a snake between 6 and 12 metres (20-40ft) long, with humps and a small head'.

Close to Norway, the mountains rise to around 1,800m (6,000ft). This is a fine area for trekking and skiing, the season for the latter sometimes lasting well into summer on the high peaks. Härjedalen was one of Sweden's earliest resort areas and has the country's oldest mountain hotel at **Fjällnäs**.

Also here are classic resorts, among which are **Tänndalen**, **Bruksvallarna** and **Ramund-berget**. These are reached via Highway 84 from Sveg.

Further north, in Jämtland, **Åre** is one of the finest modern ski resorts in the country. The town lies on the slopes of the 1,240m (4,500ft) **Åreskutan**, which towers above it. Skiers are taken by funicular railway from the town centre to a point halfway up the mountain, from where a cable car makes the rest of the trip to the summit. On Åreskutan you could be on top of the world!

Norrland and the Arctic

Norrland – the old Swedish name for 'The North' – covers the provinces of Västerbotten and Norrbotten, reaching east to the Gulf of Bothnia and the huge tract that is Lappland bordering Norway to the west – in all, a third of Sweden or so, with endless summer light and long, dark winters.

This is a remote area, with one third of it lying beyond the Arctic Circle – a fact that only acquires real significance as you travel the long moorland miles between the small communities, journeys punctuated by the gleam of lake or river, the heavy scent of the forest or sunlight catching the mountain peaks to the west.

The largest towns lie along the coast at the mouths of Sweden's great rivers since only by

river could timber be brought down to the mills on the coast. And when the roads came, it was natural that they should follow the same course.

Norrland is the heartland of the Sami, a people who have wandered this wild territory since time immemorial. They were originally called Lapps – hence Lappland – but more recently Sami has become their preferred name.

The Sami in Norrland are divided into Forest Sami and Mountain Sami. The first live

*L*appland's oldest church (at Jukkasjärvi); inside there are brilliant and unusual altar paintings.

in the forest all year round, but the Mountain Sami wander far and wide as they follow their reindeer between winter pastures in the east and summer grazing in the west.

In the past Sami culture was neglected – schoolchildren, for instance, were taught Swedish rather than Sami – but that has now changed. Sami organizations promote the language and culture, and there is an (advisory) Sami Parliament. Their great annual gathering is at the Jokkmokk market, held in the month of February (see p.94).

COAST AND RIVER

Driving north on the E4 will bring you to the coastal town of **Umeå**, Norrland's largest, with a population of 70,000. Founded in the early 17th century in Gustav II Adolf's great expansion (see p.15), since the 1970s it has become home to

---

The Sami People

The Sami have hunted wild reindeer – the only domesticated animal that can survive on the Arctic's sparse vegetation – since before the 16th century, and today this way of life acts as an effective method of reindeer management. Of the 8,000 Sami in Sweden, about a quarter make a living from reindeer.

Although life is still dictated by the reindeer, the Sami have adopted modern ways to ease their task: nowadays they herd with the aid of radios, dogs and motor cycles or snowscooters. They have kept the tradition of Sami communities, however, dividing themselves into Sami villages based on collective groups of reindeer owners who work together. The result may be that a community is not necessarily all in one place.

The Sami count, divide up their herds and mark the calves over two or three weeks during the summer, colourful occasions with lots of flying lassoes and careering reindeer. Most Sami people welcome visitors to watch – bear in mind, however, that this is not a spectacle, but the Sami way of earning a living.

Norrland's only university and emerged as a significant cultural centre. Its successful Chamber Music Festival, held each June, is now linked with the Finnish Korsholm Festival just across the Gulf.

In one of the periodic wars between Sweden and Russia, at least 1,000houses in Umeå were destroyed and, in the war of 1808-09, when Sweden lost Finland to Tzar Alexander, the town suffered heavily when Russian soldiers attacked from across the ice (old bullet holes can still be seen at the idyllic harbour of **Ratan**).

Gammlia is one of the oldest open-air museums in Sweden, dating from 1920. It also has the area's main museum, with a fine Sami exhibit and notable buildings from the region. The island of Holmön is Sweden's largest and sunniest offshore nature reserve, free of cars and with bicycles for hire.

As you head north, there are many reminders of the old industries – some now museums, others still working side by side with new, hi-tech enterprises. Church villages, from

*S*ome 2,000 Sami people still make their living from reindeer – a year-round way of life.

the days when a church served several far-flung communities, can also be seen. In **Lövånger Kyrkby**, between Umeå and Skellefteå, 100 well-restored church cottages are now used to house visitors.

Skellefteå, though largely industrial, offers the miniature world of **Lilleputlandet**. A big summer festival is celebrated in **Bonnstan Kyrkby**, which **89**

The colourful houses of Gammelstad in Luleå, where Gustav Vasa founded the original town.

has a 100-year-old steam tug, **SS Nordkust**.

From Skellefteå to **Piteå**, over the border in Norrbotten, the E4 clings to this beautiful coast, offering views of islands and headlands. **Öjebyn** has a church village dating from 1621, while Piteå, a little further north, is largely devoted to paper and pulp mills. Its mild climate has earned it the nickname of the Norrland Riviera, and the warm Gulf waters certainly attract many visitors to sea resorts such as **Pite Havsbad**, with a beach, bathing and a campsite.

As an alternative to the coast route, turn north-west on road 374 to Älvsbyn and then continue on up to Bredsel and **Storforsen**, which is claimed to be Europe's highest falls,

with a spectacular unbroken drop of 80m (265ft). Returning to Älvsbyn, take road 356 to **Boden** – Sweden's largest garrison town, a fortress built after the 1808-9 war. (Parts of Norrbotten near this border are military areas subject to entry restrictions; details are given on road signs.) From Boden, Highway 97 runs alongside Luleälven to Luleå.

The 300 islands forming the **Luleå Archipelago** are among the most beautiful in Sweden. **Luleå** itself is surrounded on all three sides by water. First founded by King Gustav II Adolf 10km (6 miles) further up the estuary, the first harbour was too small; almost 30 years later, Luleå moved to the site it occupies today. The old town, **Gammelstad**, is now a church village, with 30 old farms and 450 cottages clustered round a 15th-century granite church.

From Luleå, the E4 passes quite close to the northernmost waters of the Bothnian Gulf at **Kalix**, where the church has endured a turbulent history. Built in the 15th century, only the altar screen and font survived a fierce, early fire. After rebuilding, it was ransacked in 1716 by Russians, who used it as stables in the 1808-09 war. Victims of this war – both Swedes and Finns – are buried in the graveyard.

At **Sangis**, on the way to Haparanda, an archaeological dig in 1923 revealed a **Viking Grave**. The grave contained a warrior buried with his sword and shield, which are now in Norbotten Museum in Luleå. To the north is the Sami town of **Överkalix**.

When the treaty that ended the 1808-9 war left Sweden no access to Tornio at the mouth of the Torneälven, the Swedes promptly built **Haparanda** on the west bank – for nearly 200 years Sweden's most easterly town and today the starting point for an almost unlimited number of outdoor pastimes in the wilderness to the north.

THE INLAND WAY

There are two scenic routes for travel in Sweden's northern interior: by **Inlandsvägen** (road route, starting in Gothenburg) or **Inlandsbanan** (rail, from Mora; see p.136). Detours are easier by car, but most Swedes use the train rather like a bus, leaving it for outdoor pursuits and rejoining it later.

The **Vildmarksexpressen** (Wilderness Express) offers a special guided train tour from Östersund to Arvidsjaur, some 380km (260 miles) north, with a choice of stops and pursuits. At Gällivare the *Inlandsbanan* merges into the great east coast route from Stockholm (a long 16 hours away, best by sleeper). The route then continues to Kiruna and the border, 200km (130 miles) to the north.

Starting from Östersund by car (Highway 45), the route to Dorotea lies through Jämtland (see p.84) and endless tracts of dense forest. Both road and rail run across dozens of small islands linked by bridges and past lakes where you may see beaver and their handiwork. **91**

Most small towns between **Dorotea** and **Arvidsjaur**, 250km (175 miles) north, have a church, a local museum and possibly a craft shop, giving a taste of the past. In Dorotea itself the church has sculptures by the artists Carl Milles (see pp.32-33) and Björn Martinis.

In 1794 the principal town, **Vilhelmina**, was a church village with 241 people and 38 buildings, most of which have now been converted for summer visitors. The **Västerbottens Slöjd and Same Ätnam** (Västerbotten and Sami Crafts) is open for visits and sales. Vilhelmina is a place for folk

dancing and singing, most notably during July's festive days, which include an old-fashioned wedding. If you travel by *Vildmarksexpressen*, you may well find your arrival greeted by folk musicians, and in minutes you could even be dancing on the platform!

Several villages lie at the junctions with east-west roads, and at **Storuman** the road crosses the Blue Way (E12) from Umeå, so-called because of its many lakes. The heady panorama of lake, forest and peaks visible from Storuman's **Utkiken** ('the lookout') will show why the title was given.

Heading north again for Arvidsjaur, those with a car can divert west at Slagnäs (beyond Sorsele) on to a minor road that skirts the lovely waters of Storavan and Uddjaur to the Sami town of **Arjeplog**.

Almost surrounded by water, it lies at the junction of this small road with the Silver Road from Arvidsjaur. Apart from its splendid setting, its highlight is the **Silvermuseet**, a reminder of the silver mines nearby. It is best known for a huge collection of Sami silver and illustrations of Sami life. The church, which also displays beautiful silver, is one of Norrland's oldest, founded in 1641 by Queen Kristina.

Arvidsjaur still has the feel of a frontier town – not just because it is a training ground for army conscripts, but because it lies at the junction of five roads and, 100 years ago, became a main trading post. This pretty town of 8,000 souls has a wide main street and lakes close to the centre. **Lappstaden** is the oldest preserved church village

People head north for various reasons: botanists in search of the rich flora (left), others for walking.

in the country, with 80 Sami *kåtor* (houses) – a monument to the Forest Sami who gathered here for markets and church festivals for hundreds of years. The Sami people celebrate a festival, Storstämningshelgen, in late August.

Arvidsjaur is very much an outdoor place. **Piteälven** to the **93** north is good for white-water rafting with the magnificent **Trollforsarna** (rapids); **Trollholmen**, an island that divides the river, is popular for walks, berry-picking and picnics. The intrepid can take a course in hang-gliding; others may prefer to hire one of the old platelayer's trolleys, complete with camping equipment, and set off along the disused railway to Jörn, 70km (50 miles) to the south-east. **Vittjåksfjällen** and **Prästberget** offer good skiing.

NORTH OF THE ARCTIC CIRCLE

Just before road and railway reach **Jokkmokk** (160km/110 miles across marsh and forest to the north), you arrive at the Arctic Circle. Jokkmokk is in Sami territory and their great annual event, the **Jokkmokk Market**, first held here in 1605, takes place every year at the beginning of February.

For three days people don bright, traditional dress to meet and exchange news and have a good time. Visitors flock in to savour the Sami atmosphere and buy typical Sami handiwork, but you have to book a year ahead to be sure of a bed.

The town's **Ájtte** (museum) covers the culture and myths of the Sami as well as the hard world of the 18th- and 19th-century Swedish settlers. *Ájtte* is the Sami word for a store house, and this is indeed a fine store of artefacts, historical tableaux and exhibitions with a fascinating story to tell.

South-west of Jokkmokk on Highway 97 is **Vuollerim**, built around the excavation of a 6,000-year-old hunter settlement, and displaying well-preserved Stone Age tools and utensils. If you have an adventurous palate, Vuollerim serves the old dish of beaver.

Jokkmokk Kommun (district) is the second largest in Sweden – roughly the size of Wales or Massachusetts – and contains several vast national parks (of which **Muddus** is the closest to Jokkmokk town). It also contains the country's wildest road, **Sjöfallsleden**, which branches north-west just after Porjus and passes through awe-inspiring scenery.

The road road ends 170km (120 miles) away at **Ritsemjåkka**, high in the mountains, from where it is only another 18km (12 miles) on foot to the Norwegian Sea (Atlantic).

From **Saltuluokta**, half-way along the route, a boat also follows Sjöfallsleden. All around is the magnificent wilderness of the **Sarek**, **Padjelanta**, and the **Stora Sjöfallet National Parks** (see pp.108-9).

Rail travellers to Gällivare will arrive at its very attractive 19th-century station. In nearby Malmberget, the **Gropen** is a huge pit that yields iron ore – like a scene from Dante's Inferno. It is the source of Gällivare's prosperity. Tour buses circle deep into the mine and the **Gruvmuseet** (mining museum) shows 250 years of local mining history. Settlers lived in **Kåkstaden**, which has now been restored.

The 825m (2,700ft) summit of Gällivare's **Dundret** gives a view of just under 10 percent of the whole of Sweden. High up on one side of the mountain, a big holiday centre offers self-catering accommodation, camping facilities, restaurants and swimming pools.

From Gällivare to Kiruna, rail and road part company, the latter merging into the E10 to Kiruna via **Svappavaara**. Here, Highway 45 comes into view again to heads north-east to **Karesuando** on the Finnish border, which boasts Sweden's most northerly church.

Road and rail meet again at **Kiruna**. Until 1984 the road stopped here and the only way to Riksgränsen on the border with Norway was by rail. The road heads north along **Lake Torneträsk**, passing through some of the remotest and most beautiful scenery anywhere in the world. Experience round-the-clock sunlight here from 12 June to 4 July.

Kiruna is a mining town of 27,000 people set between two mountains packed with ore – Kirunavaara and Luossavaara – and with a lake in its centre. The first mining was by open-cast methods, but most mining today is at depth and an underground tour (by bus) is dramatic – the machines resemble great prehistoric monsters.

95

The 'father' of Kiruna must be Hjalmar Lundbohm, who helped to plan the town after his appointment as director of the newly formed mining company in 1889. Discover more about this progressive figure by visiting his home, **Hjalmar Lundbohmsgården**.

About 21km (15 miles) east of Kiruna, **Jukkasjärvi** on the Torneälven is another world, with white-water rafting in the summer and impressive winter sports. In Sami, *Jukkasjärvi* means meeting place, which is just what it was for travellers of old on their arduous treks through the great wilderness. Here is Lappland's oldest surviving wooden church, built in 1609, with a famous, brilliantly coloured altarpiece by Bror Hjort from Uppsala, an artist renowned throughout Sweden for his church paintings.

In winter, strangest of all is the **Arctic Igloo**, which was first built by local people in 1991. Each year since, as the **Arctic Hallen**, it has become a meeting place and gallery, with the Ice-Blue Bar – so-called because of the light it casts on the ice. Now, part of the igloo is used as a winter hotel for those who are unable to resist 'something different' – although local innkeeper, Nils Yngve Bergqvist, whose idea it was, also has comfortable, warm, rooms in Jukkasjärvi's Wärdshus (inn).

The still waters of Lappland's lakes make for fine fishing – and in places run deep as tradition.

At nearly 2,117m (7,000ft) **Kebnekaise**, west of Kiruna, is Sweden's highest mountain and makes a challenge even for experienced walkers. It can form the climax of a hike along **Kungsleden**, a fine route that runs 86km (60 miles) from Abisko further north with overnight stops in mountain huts. This far north, from late May to late July, the sun never sets.

Whether by road or rail, the route to **Abisko Turiststation** (Abisko Mountain Station) is beautiful, giving views over the lovely waters of Torneträsk and cutting through wilderness country with mountain peaks rising on both sides. The most noticeable heights are the twin summits that flank the deep semi-circle of **Lapporten**, the gateway to this last frontier.

Abisko has all the facilities for this outdoor life – full or self-catering accommodation, a shop, sports equipment, etc. As well as offering walking, mountain-biking and skiing, local guides are available to lead specialist weeks in topics such as botany, ornithology and railway history. Next door is the **Naturrum**, a National Park station with an informative exhibition on the **Abisko and Vadvetjåkka National Parks** (see pp.108-9).

Björkliden, some 7km or 5 miles to the north, has the highest-altitude mountain station in Sweden. At 1,228m (4,000ft), **Låktatjåkko** can attract skiers to its great 15km (10 miles) of snow trails even in high summer, a time of year when you can also see beautiful, often rare plants, some of them unique to Björkliden. In addition, the area has one of the country's best cave systems to explore. Nearby **Tornehamn** is a busy workers' settlement of the railway-building period. Its graveyard is the last resting place of those tough pioneers.

The last station in Sweden before you reach the Norwegian border is **Riksgränsen**. It is only 45 minutes by car or rail from the sea at Narvik, and you can ski there at midnight in midsummer. The settlement is home to Sven Hörnell, one of Sweden's best nature photographers, whose inspiration is all around you.

97

What to Do

Shopping

High-class department stores in Stockholm, such as NK, Åhléns and Domus, now have branches in many towns. For a bargain, look out for the words *Rea* (meaning sale) and *Extrapris* (which does not mean *extra* but a special low price). In recent years, IKEA's big stores, full of well-designed furniture and other household fittings, have become a Mecca for visitors, particularly those travelling by car. IKEA is usually sited on the outskirts of cities, and also operates an export service.

Where to Shop

Each of the three main cities has its browsing area: Gamla Stan in Stockholm, the busy Avenyn in Gothenburg and, in Malmö, a long, traffic-free zone which stretches along Södergatan from Stortorget. In addition, Gothenburg can boast the largest shopping centre in the country – the Nordstan.

Stockholm's **markets** are the colourful Östermalmstorg and Hötorget, where locals go to buy food. In Gothenburg, Feska Kyrka was built as a church but is now a fish market, while *Saluhallen* (market hall) offers shops of all kinds. Malmö's *Saluhall* is a venerable old building at Lilla Torg, complete with restaurants, delicatessens and cafés, and many of Malmö's squares have market stalls. The weekend **flea-market** in Stockholm is held in **Skärholmen Center**, which is a 20-minute ride away by Tunnelbana and claims to be the largest in Scandinavia.

What to Buy

Swedish design is hard to beat and a holiday here enables you to see it all and make your own selection. For take-home presents, Scandinavian chocolate is among the best anywhere.

Clothes: clothes for both men and women are beautifully designed, but more rarely cheap.

Hennes & Mauritz is one exception on cost and specializes in fashionable clothing at reasonable prices.

Crafts: Svenska Hemslöjd is the place to go for good quality, locally made clothing and handcrafts, normally at reasonable prices. Gold and silver are usually good, and if you spot the signs *guldsmed* or *silversmed*, you might also find original designs.

Glass: always a popular buy with visitors. The province of Småland is Sweden's 'Kingdom of Glass' (see p.47) and home to famous names such as Kosta-Boda and Orrefors, as well as many smaller companies. In most of the glassworks you can pick up what look like 'perfect' items for less than half the original price.

Porcelain: this comes to the big stores direct from the Gustavsberg factory situated outside Stockholm, and Rörstrand in Lidköping. Porcelain is by no means cheap, but the factories offer many good buys.

Textiles: like porcelain, these can be expensive, but cheaper items can sometimes be found in factories. A good place from Gothenburg is Borås in *Tygriket* (Weaver's Country).

Tax-Free Shopping

MOMS, Sweden's version of VAT, is levied on most goods. It currently stands at around 25

Whatever you're looking for, the chances are you'll be able to find it at NK. **99**

percent, but over 15,000 Swedish shops are part of a Tax-Free Shopping Scheme, aimed at non-Nordic countries residents. This enables you to reclaim most of the tax paid on goods. Participating shops carry a Tax Free sign, and with each purchase you receive a cheque for the amount of VAT, less a small handling charge. You then claim your refund at Tax Free desks at air- or seaports (or sometimes on board ship) and at border crossings or service points in Denmark, Finland and Norway.

Entertainment

For a country of just 8 million people, Sweden boasts a very large amount of music, opera, ballet and theatre in the larger cities as well as outlying areas. Theatre and concert tickets can often be bought at the kiosk at Norrmalmstorg in Stockholm.

Music, Opera & Ballet

Classical music, opera and ballet in Sweden compare with the best in the world. The **Konserthuset** is the venue for performances by the Stockholm Philharmonic Orchestra (the season runs from September to May or June), while *Sveriges Radio* (Swedish Radio) uses the **Berwaldhallen** as a base for its musical programme – the Radio Symphony Orchestra performs there regularly. Gothenburg's **Konserthuset** is home to the Gothenburg Symphony Orchestra. Malmö also has its **Konserthuset** where the Malmö Symphony Orchestra gives 50 concerts a year.

Stockholm's famous **Royal Opera House** (Operan) stages opera and ballet (late August to June); Gothenburg's **Stora Teater** is for light opera, musicals and ballet, as is **Malmö Stadsteater**, which also offers theatre performances.

For summer visitors, there is the snag that regular theatre and concert performances stop during the Swedish holiday months, from late June to late July, though music is often offered in lovely alternative settings – the **Royal Palace** and **Drottningholms Slottsteater** in Stockholm and **Liseberg** in Gothenburg – not forgetting **Malmöhus** in Malmö.

Outside the cities, Dalarna and other rural areas offer folk dancing. Scandinavians adore **jazz** and there are concerts, festivals and clubs at any time of the year.

Theatre and Cinema

For most visitors, language will prove a major problem at the theatre, as plays are more often than not preformed in Swedish. Stockholm's **Marionette Theatre** (Puppet Theatre) is one possible alternative, particularly for children.

Almost all foreign films are shown in their original language with Swedish subtitles.

Nightlife

Swedes used to go home early. Today – in the cities at least – that's all changed and nightclubs (some attached to the

Gustav III built Dramaten, Stockholm's main theatre, for the first play performed in Swedish.

bigger hotels), dance restaurants and discos may stay open to 3am, particularly on Friday and Saturday. The rural areas, however, offer little late-night entertainment except in hotels.

With the very high price of drinks, a night out is always expensive; piano bars, jazz and rock clubs or discos are often the best bet. Younger people should note that many nightclubs have surprisingly high minimum age limits.

Publications such as *Stockholm This Week* and *Malmö This Month* (free from tourist offices and some hotels and kiosks) list what's going on.

Festivals

Swedes celebrate their festivals with zest. Though fewer attend church on Sundays than in days gone by, there is still a bedrock of traditional values.

Walpurgis Night and May Day (*Valborgsmässoafton och Första Maj*): bonfires blaze for Walpurgis Night on 30 April, **102** giving a feeling of the old Viking paganism in which the festival has it roots. It is a celebration of spring and the end of the long, dark winter. In the old capital city of Uppsala, students 'sing in the spring' with traditional songs and speeches. In the evening the town is alight with torchlit parades and street parties.

Rural areas are far more likely to celebrate May Day, with outdoor picnics, games and competitions.

National Day (*Svenska Nationaldagen*): Swedes came late to the idea of a special National Day, but 6 June was chosen because the great Gustav Vasa, who founded the Vasa dynasty, became King on 6 June 1523 (see p.14). Nowadays, there are parades throughout the country and a ceremony when the King and Royal Family (Queen Silvia in Swedish national costume) present flags to organizations and individuals.

Midsommar: this is by far the biggest summer celebration in Sweden, traditionally held on the longest day, but now on the

CALENDAR OF EVENTS

Ask at local tourist offices for information on other events.

February – *Norrland:* Jokkmokk Sami Market, held since 1605.

April – *Gothenburg:* International Horse Show.

30 April/1 May – *Everywhere:* Walpurgis Night celebrations followed by May Day/Labour Day festivities.

June – *Everywhere:* Midsommar (Midsummer). Maypole dancing.
Everywhere: National Day on 6 June, marked with parades.
Stockholm: Archipelago Boat Day: steam boats to Vaxholm Island.
Motala: Vättern Round. World's largest cycle race (16,000 entries).
Dalarna: 'Church-boats' race on Lake Siljan.
Umeå: Umeå Chamber Music Festival.
Arjeplog: Lappland Music Festival.

July – *Marstrand:* International Olympic class Boat Race.
Gothenburg: Gothia Cup. Football tournament (23,000 players).
Båstad: Swedish Open and Donald Duck Youth Tennis Tournaments.
Falsterbo: Falsterbo Horse Show.
Hälsingland: Hälsingehambo – long-distance dance competition.
Bjuråker: Folk Music Festival.

August – *Everywhere:* Start of Crayfish and Sour Herring Season.
Stockholm: Water Festival and International Conference.
Västergötland: Lidköping China (Porcelain) Festival.
Vaxjö: Minnesota Day, remembering Småland emigrants.
Malmö: Swedish Derby.
Visby: Medieval Week with costumed events .
Småland: Hultsfred Rock Festival, the biggest in Sweden.
Öland: Öland Days (Harvest Festival).
Norrland: Jukkasjärvi Market from the 17th century.

September – *Norrland:* Umeå Jazz Festival (and October).

October – *Stockholm:* Lidingö. World's largest cross-country race.

December – *Stockholm:* Nobel Prize Day on 10 December.
Everywhere: St Lucia Festival, 13 December.

weekend nearest the 24th of June. Everywhere is decorated with flowers and greenery, and almost every community has its Maypole; the dancing goes on long into the night.

Pick seven different flowers from as many places, and place them under your pillow. You will dream, so they say, of your future wife or husband. Skansen in Stockholm and Liseberg in Gothenburg are excellent places to join in. Sweden's national maypole is raised in Leksand in Dalarna.

Lucia: The feast of St Lucia of Syracuse on 13 December is Sweden's great winter feast, when communities around the country choose their own Lucia, all dressed in white with a crown of candles in her hair. She is followed by a train of white-clad girls and boys and brings in a tray of coffee, saffron rolls, ginger biscuits and *glögg* (mulled wine).

Sweden's national Lucia is crowned at Skansen, and there are special Lucia concerts all over the country. The festival, like so many in Sweden, has much to do with light, the glitter and candles symbolizing a belief that, however dark December is, the light will return.

A midsummer night's dream?
Midsommar itself is dedicated to
revelling into the long, light night.

Music Festivals: like Finland,
across the Gulf of Bothnia,
Sweden specializes in summer
music festivals, with some 17
major events and many minor
gatherings held in all parts of
the country. This is a wonderful way to hear music, particularly in the north in the long,
light nights under the summer
skies. Many concerts are held
in typically Swedish venues:
castles, churches and other historic buildings. Often, the music moves out of doors, and in
the smaller communities everyone is involved.

Further details are available
from: Swedish Music Festivals, Rödhakevägen 3, S-906-
51 Umeå.

**The Start of the Crayfish and
'Sour Herring' Season** (*Kräft
och Surströmmingspremiären*)
in August is also worth noting
(see p.112).

Sports

Swedes are true outdoor people, and everywhere you should
find excellent facilities provided by the community (less often by a private club or hotel).

Equestrian Events: riding is
popular and most towns have
stables and schools. There are
many special treks for more experienced riders, ranging from
day or weekend rides around
Stockholm and Södermanland
to mountain treks in Jämtland
and Lappland, sometimes with
hunting and fishing included.
Ask for the leaflet *Equestrian
Activities*, available from the
Swedish Tourist Board in your
own country (see p.135).

There are four major tracks
for horse-racing and trotting in
Sweden: in Täby and Solvalla
(Bromma) in Stockholm, Åby
in Gothenburg, and Jägersro in
Malmö. The popular Swedish
Oaks and Derby are both held
at Jägersro, in July and August,
respectively; and Gothenburg's
International Horse Show is
held at the Scandinavium in
Gothenburg in April. **105**

Fishing: vast stretches of water make for fine fishing, in both lake, river or sea. Superb salmon can be caught in lakes Vänern and Vättern, and even in central Stockholm because the water is so pure. Freshwater fishing usually requires a permit, but sea fishing is free.

Further information may be obtained from Sveriges Sportfiske och Fiskevårdsförbund, Box 2, S-163-21 Spånga, Sweden; tel. (0) 8-795-33-50.

Golf is creeping up on tennis as one of the most popular sports in Sweden, with well over 300 courses. Most are private clubs, charging green fees, and some have special rules for visitors (for example, requiring an official handicap).

In summer, in the north you can enjoy the rare experience of playing golf under the Midnight Sun. Further information is available from the Swedish Golf Federation, Post Box 84, S-182-11 Danderyd, Sweden; tel. (0) 8-622-15-00.

Skiing: in Sweden everyone skis just as soon they can walk, and cross-country and downhill runs abound. One of the best resorts is Åre in Jämtland (see p.86), and in many areas you can ski all year round. Ski-touring is also popular.

Spectator Sports: indoor and outdoor spectator sports, both at international and local level, include everything from tennis and golf to football, riding and boat racing. Handball is popular, and some of the biggest tournaments are held in Stockholm. In June the capital plays host to one of Europe's biggest marathons. Dundret mountain at Gällivare in Lappland is the scene of a hang-gliding festival in early July.

The Swedish Tourist Board (see p.135) publishes a useful annual booklet, *Coming Events in Sweden*, listing all the main events and venues.

Tennis: in the wake of Borg, Wilander and Edberg, there are many indoor and outdoor courts for public use throughout Sweden. Hotels may have tennis courts, but they are not a standard feature.

Båstad on Skåne's south-west coast is the venue for the Swedish Open and the Donald Duck Club Junior Tournament (both held in July). Stockholm's Globe Arena hosts the Stockholm Open (October).

Walking: walking takes pride of place alongside skiing as the Swede's preferred outdoor activity. Most popular are long-distance upland paths, such as Kungsleden in Lappland (see p.97), which attract hundreds every weekend, yet never become crowded. There are also forest tracks and space where *allemansrätt*, the law that allows wandering at will, can be enjoyed. You'll find mountain huts on most routes, and elsewhere wilderness camping is the attraction, especially in the National Parks (see p.108).

Watersports: there are limitless possibilities, from swimming and canoeing to sailing and fishing. In summer, lakes Vänern and Vättern are dotted with boats, swimmers and anglers. Every town has its indoor and/or outdoor swimming pool, plus a growing number of special adventure pools.

Windsurfing and water skiing are increasingly popular, as is white-water rafting, particularly in the north. All over Sweden you can hire motor and sailing boats. Ask for the leaflets *Boat Hire* and *Canoeing Centres* from the Swedish Tourist Board (see p.108).

*T*est your skills against the experts: join in the tennis fervour at tournaments in Båstad.

National Parks

Sweden's first four National Parks, all in Lappland, were opened in 1909. Largely wild, mountain terrain with lakes and rivers, they cover huge stretches of land. The largest, **Padjelanta**, covers 198,400ha (some 490,250 acres) – a greater area than Lake Vänern.

The main objective of National Parks is to preserve Sweden's varied wild landscapes, and there are now 22 parks spread throughout the country, from Lappland to Skåne. They also offer the chance for everyone to enjoy the peace and tranquility of water, landscape and wildlife.

One or two parks are total wilderness, where the Swedes indulge their passion for getting back to nature and where you can wander for days with-

During the summer, Swedes are at their happiest either when on or in the water.

out seeing another soul. Others have footpaths, walking trails, accommodation and even cable cars. **Sånjfället** in Härjedallen has a bear population, and on the island of **Blå Jungfrun**, in the Kalmar Sound in Småland, legend tells that witches appear on the night of Maundy Thursday.

Further information is available from the Swedish Environmental Protection Agency, S-171-85 Solna, Sweden; tel. (0) 8-799-10-00, and Svenska Turist Föreningen (STF), Box 25, Drottninggatan 31, S-101-20 Stockholm; tel. (0) 8-790-31-00; fax: (0) 8-20-13-32.

Svenska runs the country's youth hostels, mountain stations and huts, which vary from basic shelters to large mountain stations with hotel-standard comforts. STF also owns 460 guest harbours (moorings).

Children

No child will go short of a Swedish **beach**, even in the heart of Stockholm, where the waters – salt or fresh – are pristine clean. The long west coast running north and south of Gothenburg provides endless swimming, as do the south coasts closer to Denmark. The sheltered waters of the Gulf of Bothnia are referred to as the Swedish Riviera.

Several country hotels and camping sites also have their own pools, plus sports and various **play areas**. In addition, there are numerous public play areas called *Parlek*, which provide bikes and tricycles, buckets and spades and other toys, as well as paid play workers and tea and coffee.

The two great **amusement parks** in Sweden are Gröna Lund in Stockholm and Liseberg in Gothenburg. In the capital there is also the **open-air museum**, Skansen, with its fascinating old workshops.

Fjärilshus (Butterfly House) at Haga Park in Stockholm has hundreds of tropical butterflies flying free. The **Marionettmuseet** (Puppet Theatre Museum) offers glove puppets and marionettes as well as masks. For a journey into space, try **Cosmonova** (only 15 minutes away **109**

*S*tockholm's Tjemilen *race – when women dress up and run a 'Swedish mile' (10km or 6 miles).*

by Tunnelbana to the *Universitetet* station).

Some **castles** also now have their own children's sections. **Läckö**, north of Lidköping on Lake Vänern, has a children's museum, and **Tidö Slott**, north of Mälaren, has a huge collection of dolls and toys. Around 130km (90 miles) south of Stockholm in Södermanland is **Kolmården Wild Animal Park**, with a pets' corner and more than 100 animal species.

Malmö's and Gothenburg's **Little Trains** are a good way to get around, and old **trams** in Gothenburg are also great fun. **Almviks Djurfrititdsgård** (or Almvik Children's Farm) is a genuine Skåne farm that was brought into the middle of a Malmö housing estate. Nearby is **Ak-va-Kul**, the largest water park in Scandinavia. Over on the east coast, **Saga Town** in Vimmerby is a celebration of the works of children's writer Astrid Lindgren (see p.47).

In the north, there are three different types of **zoos** at Östersund, Junsele and Lycksele, and unusual museums, such as the **Teknikens Hus** (Technical House) in Luleå, which keeps children occupied with hands-on exhibitions. If you're skiing, winter resorts such as Åre (see p.86) have good facilities for children.

Note for parents: travel on Stockholm's buses is free of charge for one parent if you have one or more children in a pram or pushchair. You get on and off the buses using the middle doors, which are wide enough for double pushchairs.

Eating Out

It has become easier to sample traditional Swedish dishes in restaurants because, in a sense, eating out has come full circle. Originally, most restaurants offered Swedish cuisine, but during the 1980s the restaurant scene went through something of a sea change when, in the cities certainly, it was easier to find French, Chinese or Italian than local dishes. Now, some Swedish restaurants have regained the confidence to serve their native cuisine.

WHERE TO EAT

Stockholm has more than 700 restaurants covering food from some 30 countries. In Skåne the motto is: 'Plenty of food, good food, and food at the right time', so it is no surprise that Malmö claims to have more restaurants per head than anywhere else in Sweden.

Most top-class restaurants, which may be part of a hotel or independently owned, have the expense-account diner as their clientele and can cost a lot, but there is a growing number of smaller, less expensive places, especially for lunch.

On the whole, the Swedes eat earlier than other nations. Lunch is served from 11am, the evening meal usually at 6pm. Bigger restaurants, city hotels and motels expect their guests to arrive later, and many cafés and dance restaurants serve food well into the night.

For a typically Swedish offering, try one of the many *korvkiosk* along the city streets. These covered food stalls serve plain but good fare: sausage (which is what *korv* means), grilled chicken and, nowadays, the inevitable hamburgers and chips. While in Stockholm pay a visit to the *Saluhall*, an atmospheric food hall on Östermalmstorg where delicatessen stalls selling meat, cheese, fish and cakes are complemented by a number of good cafés and restaurants.

Note: Some restaurants will charge a fee of 5-10 Skr for leaving your coat in the cloak room, which you are obliged to do, anyway.

WHAT TO EAT

Hotel **breakfasts** (*frukost*) are a less lavish version of the *smörgåsbord* cold table (see p.114), but are still enough to keep anyone going for most of the day. The *dagens rätt* **lunch** menu is also good value.

The Swedes like the natural products of river and forest, particularly fish (a speciality in Gothenburg) and meats such as venison and reindeer. Foods typical of midsummer are herring and boiled new potatoes flavoured with dill (a popular herb) followed by a gleaming heap of fresh strawberries.

One dish that you may like to try is *gravad lax* (delicately marinaded **salmon**) – many people find this preferable to smoked salmon. It is always served with a dill sauce. The ubiquitous boiled potatoes ar-

---

The Crayfish and 'Sour Herring' Season
(*Kräft och Surströmmingspremiären*)

Swedes have an understandable passion for crayfish and – to those not born to it – an inexplicable addiction to *surströmming* (fermented herring), which replaces crayfish further north.

The crayfish season starts in August with a grand party, indoors or out. Sporting comic hats and paper bibs, guests sit at a long table lit by paper lanterns and loaded with glasses, aquavit and delicious crayfish. Eating is punctuated by toasts, traditional songs and toasting songs, including the best known of all, *Helan går* ... (something equivalent to 'down it in one'), the intricacies of which are better attempted than explained.

Surströmming is a dish made of Baltic herring, salted and set aside for a long time, then put into sealed tins. With the herring, the brave eat *tunnbröd* (thin bread), raw onions and *mandelpotatis* (small, sweetish, almond-shaped potatoes). Connoisseurs claim that milk is the correct drink.

To many Swedes – and all foreigners – the downing of this overpowering meal is virtually a test of machismo.

rive with most meals, and are also sprinkled with dill.

Fiskbullar (**fish balls**) are also popular, as are *köttbullar* (**meat balls**). Two typically Swedish dishes, which hark back to the days when nothing was allowed to go to waste, are *Janssons Frestelse* (**Jansson's Temptation**), a tangy mixture of potato, onion and anchovy, and **pyttipana** (literally, 'put in the pan'), a delicious hotch-potch of leftovers all fried up together. In many rural areas of Sweden you can still enjoy these traditional dishes, which are known by the general term *husmanskost* (home cooking).

There is also a selection of delicious **buns** (*bullar*) – at their best in the baker's shop at Skansen. *Semlor*, once a tradi-tional Shrove Tuesday delight eaten before the long fast, is now popular enough to appear immediately after Christmas. With a filling of almond paste and whipped cream, the buns are correctly served up in a dish of hot milk with a sprinkling of cinnamon.

Våfflor (**waffles**), thought by many to be North American,

Reason to smile – waffles and hjortron (cloudberries) are perfect for a sunny winter's day.

were in fact introduced there by Scandinavian emigrants. In their original homeland they are simply mouth-watering.

If you're visiting Småland and 'The Glass Country' (see pp.44-8), look out for **Hyttsill Evenings**. These continue an old tradition from times when the glassblowing hall was a **113** social as well as a work place for local people, who cooked herring beside the furnaces. The pudding that follows is the traditional Småland delicacy, curd cake with sour cherry or strawberry jam, eaten in the glow of the furnace, and to the sound of traditional music and story-telling.

Fruits of the Forest

The country's forests provide **mushrooms** (*svamp*) and **wild berries**, which *allemansrätt* (see p.107) allows you to pick anywhere, so that it is almost fashionable to return with stained fingers after a summer weekend. A profuse variety of wild berries grows in Scandinavia, from *smultron* (**wild strawberries**) to *hjortron* (**cloudberries**) – causing endless confusion as the different countries all have their own names for the different types!

Smörgåsbord

It is a tribute to the rise of Swedish cuisine that people all **114** over the world can say the word *smörgåsbord*, the great cold-table buffet common to all three Scandinavian nations.

The *smörgåsbord* is a substantial, celebratory meal that's served on Sundays and special occasions. It has also begun to appear on hotel menus as something typically Swedish.

It starts with herring of various sorts, shrimps, salmon and other fish. Next come the cold meats and cheeses, with caviar, eggs and different salads. This is followed by hot dishes, even though it is a 'cold' table, with fruit or pudding and coffee to follow. The farming area of Skåne in the south, as guardian of the old way of life, claims to make the best *smörgåsbord*. Hotel breakfasts are a smaller version of the meal.

DRINKS

To drink with a meal, there are three strengths of beer: light (Class I), ordinary (Class II) and export (Class III). You can purchase wine for not much more than 35Skr in the state alcohol stores, *Systembolaget*, but restaurants multiply that by three or more in an effort, so some say, to keep beer and spirit prices more reasonable. Aquavit is a must with herring at the start of the *smörgåsbord*.

Aquavit

Most European countries have their own favourite firewater; in Scandinavia it is Aquavit (*Akvavit*) – the water of life – which is also sometimes called *snaps*. Sweden's most popular brand is *Skåne*.

Straight aquavit is distilled from potatoes or barley. What makes each brand different is what goes into it afterwards – juniper, coriander, or perhaps myrtle, or whatever distinctive flavour the distiller can devise.

Aquavit is served in tiny glasses and quaffed ice cold (many families cool it in the freezer rather than the fridge, or in the snow outside at a winter *stuga*). It is drunk at the beginning of a meal, usually as an accompaniment to fish – ideally the herring that starts a *smörgåsbord* (see previous page). Raising your glass in a toast (see p.126) is an essential part of the ancient ritual of drinking aquavit.

Many experiment with their own flavours, putting a leaf or sprig of herbs into a half bottle and leaving it to mature. Some make their own, so if you're offered a selection of aquavit in a private house, don't enquire about the brand. Home distilling is an open secret.

All that's required for a good Swedish evening – aquavit, beer and smoked sausage.

To Help You Order ...

May I have the menu, please.	**Kan jag få matsedeln, tack.**
What do you recommend?	**Vad rekommenderar ni?**
Do you have any vegetarian dishes?	**Har ni några vegetariska rätter?**
I'd like to pay.	**Får jag betala.**

beetroot	**rödbetor**	prawns	**räkor**
carrots	**morötter**	reindeer	**ren**
cauliflower	**blomkål**	roast beef	**rostbiff**
chicken	**kyckling**	roast lamb	**lammstek**
egg dishes	**äggrätter**	salmon	**lax**
ham	**skinka**	smoked Baltic	
mushrooms	**svamp**	herring	**böckling**
octopus	**bläckfisk**	spinach	**spenat**
onions	**lök**	tomatoes	**tomater**
peas	**ärtor**	trout	**forell**
pike	**gädda**	tuna	**tonfisk**
pork chop	**fläskkotlett**	venison	**rådjur**

... and Read the Menu

bakverk	pastries	**ost**	cheese
drycker	drinks	**pasталätter**	pasta
efterrätter	desserts	**risrätter**	rice
fisk	fish	**sallader**	salad
frukt	fruit	**skaldjur**	seafood
från grillen	grilled (broiled)	**soppor**	soups
fågel	poultry	**smårätter**	snacks
förrätter	first course	**smörgåsar**	sandwiches
glass	ice-cream	**smörgåsbord**	cold table
grönsaker	vegetables	**varmrätter**	main course
huvudrätter	main course	**vilt**	game
kött	meat	**vinlista**	wine list

BLUEPRINT
for a
Perfect Trip

An A–Z Summary of Practical Information

An appropriate Swedish translation is given after most main entries, usually in the singular. You will find this vocabulary useful when asking for information or assistance.

A

ACCOMMODATION (*logi*) (See also CAMPING on p.120, YOUTH HOSTELS on p.139 and the list of RECOMMENDED HOTELS starting on p.65)

Swedish hotels (*hotell*) are almost invariably warm, comfortable and well run. Many higher-grade hotels have saunas and plunge pools and some also have swimming pools.

They are also among Europe's higher-priced hotels and the secret to keeping costs reasonable is to choose your time. Hotels are geared to business travel and during slack periods – early summer to mid- or late-August and at weekends – they slash their rates (sometimes by as much as 50%). Always ask about discounts and special rates, including the special Stockholm, Gothenburg and Malmö packages. In addition, many Swedish hotel chains offer special rates, usually in summer. Sweden Hotels, for instance, has a 'Scandinavian Bonus-pass' which carries 15-50% discounts (usually May-September and winter weekends) at their hotels throughout the country. (It also has a reciprocal scheme with hotels in Norway, Denmark and Finland.) Svenska Turistförening hotels (see p.139) also offer good value.

Before making plans – and certainly bookings – ask for a copy of the Swedish Travel Board's Council's (see p.135) excellent *Hotels* booklet, which lists hotels and gives details of all schemes.

Self-catering accommodation is also good. A Swedish family may rent out its own *stuga* (traditional wooden holiday house). Tour operators and tourist offices offer self-catering packages and there are 350 purpose-built holiday villages, with canoes, bikes, boats, etc. for hire.

AIRPORTS *(flygplatser)*
Sweden's three main airports are Arlanda (serving Stockholm and Uppsala), Landvetter (Gothenburg), and Sturup (Malmö), the last mainly for internal flights. All have airport coaches to and from their respective city's Central Station. Taxis are more expensive. SAS operates a limousine service to any address in the surrounding area, which is costly for a single passenger but less so if sharing.

Arlanda has four terminals: three domestic and one overseas, with inter-terminal buses. There are self-service cafés, a restaurant, duty-free and Swedish food shops, a hotel, a tourist/accommodation office and car-hire desks. Arlanda is 42km (26 miles) from the centre of Stockholm. The airport bus stops at Ulriksdal (northern suburbs), Skt Eriksplan (inner city) and Terminalen at Central Station, where there is a taxi-rank for onward journeys. There are also special bus and taxi offers to and from hotels. Arlanda tel. (0) 8-797-60-00.

Landvetter is smaller, with a good, small hotel, duty-free shop and self-service restaurant. Situated 24km (17 miles) from Gothenburg, there is an airport bus which takes around 30 minutes to and from the centre. Landvetter tel. (0) 31-94-10-0.

Malmö-Sturup is 30km (21 miles) from the city centre (roughly 40 minutes). It has one terminal with a restaurant, cafés and duty-free shop, and there is an airport hotel. Sturup tel. (0) 40-50-10-00.

B

BICYCLE HIRE/RENTAL
Sweden's uncrowded roads make cycling popular, and bicycles can be rented almost anywhere; the local tourist office usually has details. Typical cost: 80Skr per day or 300-400Skr per week. Further

details from: Svenska Turistförening, Box 25, S-101-20 Stockholm; tel. (0) 8-790-31-00, and Cykelfrämjandet, Box 6027, S-102-31; tel. (0) 8-32-16-80, which publishes a 'Swedish Cycling' guide in English.

C

CAMPING (camping)

There are 750 graded camping sites, often by lake or sea, with boats, canoes and bikes for hire, and maybe riding, mini-golf and tennis on offer. Most are open in June-August, some earlier but not necessarily with full facilities. Around 200 sites open in winter-sports areas.

You must have a Camping Card to use Swedish camp sites, available for around 60Skr at the first camp site at which you stay, but not required if you hold an International Camping Card. Note: Only propane gas (eg. Primus) is allowed in Sweden, *never* butane.

Sweden's access tradition, *allemansrätt* (Everyone's Right; see p.107) allows you one-night's camping anywhere, without permission (even on private property), but campers should not stay too close to houses, damage their surroundings or leave litter. Instead of tents or caravans many sites have 2-6-bed log cabins equipped with cooking facilities and utensils, but not bedding (bring sleeping bags).

Further details are available in the brochure *Camping in Sweden*, available from the Swedish Travel Board (see p.135).

CAR HIRE/RENTAL (biluthyrning)

(See also DRIVING on p.123 and MONEY MATTERS on p.131)
Most big companies, such as Avis, Hertz, Budget and Europcar have offices in airports and larger towns, with a wide range of cars. Special rates are usually available between mid-June and mid-August, and weekends throughout the year. Always ask about discounts, particularly packages connected with domestic air and rail travel. You can often rent a car in one place and return it to another.

Most companies ask for a **deposit**, which is usually a credit card imprint. The legal minimum **driving age** in Sweden is 18, but to hire a car you usually need to have held a licence for three years, so in practice the minimum age is **21**. Check up on **Collision Damage Reducer** (not 'Waiver' as in other countries), which costs around 60Skr a day and limits damage liability to 500Skr.

CLIMATE and CLOTHING

Most of Sweden has a continental climate with a medium to large temperature difference between summer and winter. Shorts and T-shirts are often the norm in Stockholm during the summer, when everyone swims. Temperatures above 20°C (70°F) are not unusual.

The climate can be particularly variable in the west, which has more rain than inland or eastern Sweden. Long hours of sunlight can mean high temperatures in the north, and swimsuit skiing on the northern border at Björkliden, near Riksgränsen, is not unknown. Conversely, in the depth of winter, temperatures in the north can sink as low as -30°C (-22°F).

The brief northern spring turns swiftly to summer around the end of May, but by the end of September autumn is turning into winter. The seasons in the south are more even. Autumn, with light frost at night and the glowing sun on the changing colours of the foliage by day, is beautiful. From Gothenburg to Malmö, the west coast climate is moderated by an open sea which rarely freezes.

The chart below shows the average daily maximum and minimum temperatures and number of rainy days each month in Stockholm.

	J	F	M	A	M	J	J	A	S	O	N	D
Max °F	31	31	37	45	57	65	70	66	58	48	38	33
Max °C	-1	-1	3	7	14	18	21	19	14	9	3	1
Min °F	23	22	26	32	41	49	55	53	46	39	31	26
Min °C	-5	-6	-3	0	5	9	13	12	8	4	-1	-3
Days of rainfall	10	7	6	7	7	8	9	10	9	9	10	11

Clothing. It is a good idea to be prepared for changes and to wear several layers. Even in summer keep a sweater and waterproof covering to hand, as well as T-shirts, shorts or a skirt and cotton trousers. The north always demands warm outer wear.

Winter also calls for layers. Houses are warm and the custom is to leave heavy clothing just inside the front door (or in your hotel cloak-room). Walkers should take good walking boots and a rucksack. Winter essentials are headgear, preferably wool or fur, and two pairs of gloves or mitts (thin/thick). Good footwear is necessary for snow and slushy streets. If you plan to be out of doors a lot, a thermal layer is advised. For evenings, Swedes dress informally, casual but smart.

COMMUNICATIONS

Post Offices (*postkontor*). Swedish postboxes are yellow. Post offices usually open 9am-6pm Mon-Fri, 10am 1pm Saturday. Some branches close on Saturday in July.

Telephones (*telefon*)/**Faxes**. Swedish post offices do not have telephones but there are plenty of payphones in stations, streets, hotels and other public institutions, as well as special Telegraph Offices (marked *Telia*), which also send faxes. (Most hotels should be able to send faxes as well.) Automatic payphones are always cheaper than those in hotels. Credit-card phones (indicated by a CCC sign) are also plentiful. Calls within Europe cost around 7Skr a minute.

COMPLAINTS

The Swedish sense of fair play makes complaining a rare event. In a restaurant or hotel, a quiet word with the manager is usually enough. Serious complaints about hotels or other major services should be directed to tourist offices or to the appropriate travel authority.

CRIME (See also EMERGENCIES on p.125 and POLICE on p.133)

Sweden is one of the safest countries in the world. It is safe to walk in cities at night, but on Friday and Saturday evenings you may meet groups of revellers – who are likely to be noisy rather than dangerous – and Stockholm's *Tunnelbana* (underground) can be boisterous.

You may prefer a taxi. Should anything happen to you, contact the police. The emergency number **90-000** is free from payphones.

CUSTOMS and ENTRY FORMALITIES

Europeans and North Americans need only a valid passport to enter Sweden. Visitors from the UK need only a British Visitor's Passport. Other nationalities should check with local Swedish Consulates.

Duty-free. Allowances into **Sweden** are as follows: for residents of European countries 200 cigarettes or 50 cigars or 250g tobacco, 1l of wine and 1l of spirits; for residents of non-European countries 400 cigarettes or 100 cigars or 500g tobacco, 1l wine and 1l spirits. When returning to your own country you may take the following: **Australia**: 250 cigarettes or 250g tobacco, 1l wine or spirits; **Canada**: 200 cigarettes and 50 cigars and 400g tobacco, 1.1l wine or spirits or 8.5l beer; **New Zealand**: 200 cigarettes or 50 cigars or 250g tobacco, 4.5l wine or beer and 1.1l spirits; **Republic of Ireland**: 200 cigarettes or 50 cigars or 250g tobacco, 2l wine or 1l spirits; **South Africa**: 400 cigarettes and 50 cigars and 250g tobacco, 2l wine and 1l spirits; **UK**: 200 cigarettes or 50 cigars or 250g tobacco, 2l still wine and 1l spirits; **USA**: 200 cigarettes and 100 cigars and 2kg tobacco, 1l wine or spirits.

Currency Restrictions. There is no restriction on the amount you can take into Sweden, but no more than 6,000Skr may be taken out.

D

DRIVING IN SWEDEN

Swedish roads are well-maintained and uncrowded and outside the cities driving is easy despite the small number of motorways.

Speed limits. Speed limits, shown on road signs, are usually 50kmh (30mph) in built-up areas; 70kmh (43mph) on trunk roads; 90 or 110kmh (55 or 70mph) on motorways. Caravan limits are lower.

Documents. To drive your own car in Sweden you need: a national or international driving licence; car registration documents; green card or other valid third party (or comprehensive) insurance.

Driving rules. Drive on the right, pass on the left and, unless road signs indicate otherwise, give way to traffic approaching from the right. Traffic on a roundabout usually has right of way. Seatbelts are obligatory for everyone in the car. Dipped headlights (which should be adjusted on right-hand-drive cars) must be used day and night.

Drink-driving laws are strict and well enforced. Drinking when in charge of a car attracts very high fines, or even a jail sentence. The best course is never to drink if you're driving. In the effort to stamp out drink-driving, police carry out fairly frequent spot checks on licences and vehicles.

Accidents and Breakdowns. Contact either the local police or *Larmtjänst*, run by Swedish insurance companies, which operates a 24-hour recovery service. Telephone numbers are listed in Swedish telephone directories.

Serious accidents, especially if there are injuries, warrant use of the **90-000** emergency number for the police. Although it is not mandatory to call the police to an accident, even if damage is slight drivers must give their name and contact address to others involved before leaving the scene. Drivers who do not stop after an accident are liable to a fine or, in certain cases, imprisonment.

International pictographs are widely used, although you may see some signs in Swedish.

biljettautomat	ticket machine
bussfil	bus lane
busshållplats	bus stop
ej genomfart	no through traffic
privat parkering	private parking
körkort	driving licence
car registration papers	**besiktningsinstrument**
Please check the oil/tyres/battery.	**Kan ni kontrollera oljan/däcken/batteriet, tack.**
I've broken down.	**Bilen har gått sönder.**
There's been an accident.	**Det har hänt en olycka.**

Distance

| km | 0 | 1 | 2 | 3 | 4 | 5 | 6 | | 8 | | 10 | | 12 | | 14 | | 16 |

Fluid measures

US gals 0 ... 5 ... 10

imp. gals 0 ... 5 ... 10

litres 0 5 10 20 30 40 50

ELECTRIC CURRENT

Swedish electricity is 220 volts AC, and requires standard two-pin, round continental plugs. Visitors should bring their own adaptors.

EMBASSIES and CONSULATES (*ambassad; konsulat*)

Britain: Skapögata 6-8, S-155-27 Stockholm; tel. (0) 8-667-01-40.

Republic of Ireland: Östermalmsgatan 97, S-114-69 Stockholm; tel. (0) 8-661-80-05/-661-74-09.

USA: Strandvägen 101, 115-89 Stockholm; tel. (0) 8-783-53-00.

Most embassies open 8am-4pm, but there is usually someone on duty 24 hours a day. Telephone in advance if in doubt.

EMERGENCIES (See also POLICE on p.133)

Radio Sweden broadcasts vital messages to travellers in Sweden. The station can be heard on medium wave 1179KHz (254m) and in the Stockholm area on FM 89.6MHz, and messages should be sent to a broadcasting organization in your country of origin, Interpol, or the appropriate embassy in Sweden (see EMBASSIES AND CONSULATES above, and see also MEDIA on p.128)

For the **police**, **fire brigade** or **ambulance**, dial **90-000** from anywhere in Sweden. Calls are free from pay phones.

ETIQUETTE (See also T ipping on p.134)

The most useful word is *tack* (thank-you), which is used very often, partly because there is no precise equivalent for 'please' in Swedish. Swedes are punctual and the idea of '7.30 for 8' does not exist. When drinks are served, it is polite to wait for the host/hostess to raise the glass with a *Skål!* (Cheers!) or *Välkommen och Skål!* (Welcome and Skål!). Eye contact is important, both with your glass raised for *Skål* and immediately after the first taste.

If invited to a private house, it is customary to take flowers to your hostess and, to be quite correct, to phone the following day to say *Tack för senast* (literally, 'thanks for last time').

In contrast, all Scandinavians have a relaxed attitude to nudity, particularly in the sauna (*bastu*). Even so, men and women usually use the *bastu* separately (unless with family or close friends), perhaps meeting afterwards in their bathrobes to cool off with a beer.

If you're travelling with children, note that spanking or smacking children is now illegal in Sweden, and if you do so in public you are likely to come up against indignant, law-abiding citizens.

G

GAY and LESBIAN TRAVELLERS

Sweden is one of the world's most progressive countries when it comes to Gay Rights. Since 1988 government legislation has granted gay relationships the same status as heterosexual marriages and the state has given financial support to gay organizations. Information and advice can be obtained from the Swedish Federation for Lesbian and Gay Rights: RSFL (*Riksförbundet för Sexuellt Likaberättigade*), Stockholms Gay-hus, Sveavägen 57. (Postal address: Förbundskansli, Box 350, S-101-26 Stockholm); tel. (0) 8-736-02-13.

GUIDES (*guide*) and TOURS

English is Sweden's second language, which makes it easy to get an English-speaking guide. German-speaking guides are almost as plentiful. Bus or boat tours are multi-lingual, as are those in some museums and other places of interest. Local tourist offices can also make bookings for tours and guides, or tell you where to book.

LANGUAGE

School children learn English from the age of nine, and most Swedes speak excellent English, a little less so in remote areas. German is the next choice of language and is spoken by many (particularly in the tourist industry). City menus often give English translations.

The word *turist* in Swedish (as in *Abisko Turiststation*; see p.97) means 'tourist' in the Scandinavian sense of someone who travels in remote areas under his or her own power, not 'tourist' as in English.

Swedish is not easy to pronounce and the language has three extra vowels. They are å, ä, and ö (listed in the phone book as the last three letters of the alphabet).

The words and expressions below may be of some use (see also the USEFUL EXPRESSIONS on the front cover flap of this guide).

USEFUL EXPRESSIONS

big/small	**stor/liten**	next/last	**nästa/sista**
quick/slow	**snabb/långsam**	good/bad	**bra/dålig**
hot/cold	**varm/kall**	early/late	**tidig/sen**
heavy/light	**tung/lätt**	cheap/expensive	**billig/dyr**
open/shut	**öpen/stängd**	near/far	**nära/långt (bort)**
right/wrong	**rätt/fel**		
old/new	**gammal/ny**	here/there	**här/där**

DAYS OF THE WEEK*

Sunday	**söndag**	Thursday	**torsdag**
Monday	**måndag**	Friday	**fredag**
Tuesday	**tisdag**	Saturday	**lördag**
Wednesday	**onsdag**		

127

MONTHS*

January	**januari**	July	**juli**
February	**februari**	August	**augusti**
March	**mars**	September	**september**
April	**april**	October	**oktober**
May	**maj**	November	**november**
June	**juni**	December	**december**

*The names of days and months aren't capitalized in Swedish.

LOST PROPERTY (*hittegods*)

Stockholm: Main Lost Property Office (*hittegodsexpedition*);
tel. (0) 8-769-30-75
Stockholm Local Traffic Office (SL);
tel. (0) 8-600-10-00, for property lost on buses,
Tunnelbana and local trains.

Gothenburg: Lost Property; tel. (0) 31-61-8-00

Malmö: Lost Property; tel. (0) 40-20-10-00

If you lose property elsewhere, first retrace your steps and then try
the main police, railway or bus station.

M

MEDIA

Radio and Television. *Sveriges Radio* (Radio Sweden) and *Sveriges
Television* (Swedish Television) are the main companies, though
there are now also local radio and various commercial television
channels. *Sveriges Radio* broadcasts regular 30-minute programmes
of news and information in English, which can be heard over most of
Sweden on medium wave 1179KHz (254m), and also in the Stockholm area on FM 89.6MHz. Further details are available from Radio
Sweden International, S-105-10 Stockholm; tel. (0) 8-784-00, or
from many hotels. Gothenburg local radio also has a daily half-hour

English news and tourist information programme. In addition to Swedish channels, most hotels carry English-language satellite channels such as Super Channel and CNN, plus German-language channels direct from Germany.

Newspapers and Magazines (*tidning; tidskrift*). Sweden's main daily newspapers are *Svenska Dagbladet*, *Dagens Nyheter* and *Göteborgs Posten* (broadsheets), and *Expressen* and *Aftonbladet* (tabloids), all in Swedish. English-language newspapers are on sale in kiosks and central stations. Stockholm's Kulturhuset (Culture House) has a selection of English-language newspapers to read on the premises, as does the City Library in Gothenburg. Stockholm also has a visitors' newspaper, *Stockholm this Week*, and Malmö has *Malmö this Month*.

MEDICAL CARE (See also EMERGENCIES on p.125)

No vaccinations are needed for Sweden, nor does the country have the equivalent of the general-practice surgery.

If you become ill, ask your hotel to call a doctor who is affiliated to *Försäkringskassan* (Swedish National Health Service). If you are able, go to the casualty department, *Akutmottagning*, at a hospital, or *Vårdcentral* (health centre) in more rural areas. Take your passport with you for identification. Hospital visits cost 90Skr (200Skr for the casualty department). Take a doctor's prescription for medicines to any chemist (*apotek*). These are open during shopping hours.

All-night chemists can be found in the following places:

Stockholm: CW Scheele, Klarabergsgatan 64; tel. (0) 8-24-82-80.

Gothenburg: Vasen, Götgatan 12; tel. (0) 31-80-44-10.

Malmö: Gripen, Bergsgatan 48; tel. (0) 40-19-21-10.

Dental treatment. *Tandläkare* means dental surgery. Emergency services in larger cities are shown on health 'blue' pages of the Business telephone directory.

Sweden has a reciprocal agreement for medical treatment with Britain and most European countries, which means citizens of those countries are entitled to the same emergency service as Swedes.

MONEY MATTERS

Currency. Swedish currency is the *krona* (or crown, plural *kronor*), made up of 100 *öre*. It is abbreviated kr, Skr, or SEK (banker's abbreviation). Coins come in 50 öre, 1 krona, and 5 and 10 kronor. Bank notes are 20, 50, 100, 1,000 and 10,000 kronor.

Exchange facilities. You can change currency at: airports; the Central Stations in Malmö, Stockholm and Gothenburg; almost all commercial and savings banks; post offices; branches of 'Forex' (bureaux de change); hotels; and some department stores.

Credit Cards. Most well-known credit cards are accepted. Shops and restaurants usually indicate which they take. Individual banks often have links to particular cards for currency exchange facilities.

Traveller's Cheques. Banks and hotels will change traveller's cheques or cash, but banks usually give a better rate. Shops accept traveller's cheques for purchases.

PLANNING YOUR BUDGET

All prices given are approximate. In this large country, different areas have different prices, and Stockholm is usually the most expensive.

Car hire: Prices vary tremendously: small car (eg VW Golf): weekend, incl. 200km (140 miles) 600Skr; week (5-7 days), incl. 1,000km (700 miles) 3,000Skr. Large car (eg SAAB 9,000 CDE): weekend, incl. 200km (140 miles) 1,000Skr; week (5-7 days), incl. 1,000km (700 miles) 5,000Skr. In both cases: each extra km costs 1Skr. Weekend means noon on Friday to noon on Monday.

Food and (especially) **alcoholic drink** are expensive. Self-caterers are advised to bring in a car-load of food and other necessities.

Guides: Guides are not cheap: around 650Skr for three hours, and 200Skr or more for each additional hour, plus booking fee of 150Skr.

Hotels: Average rates for hotels (per night) can be divided into three categories (based on two people sharing a double room and including full breakfast): under 1,100Skr; 1,100-1,800Skr; over 1,800Skr.

Prices at the lower end may be well below 1,100Skr, but equally, prices at the top end may rise considerably above 1,800Skr. These are full rates. Visitors can take advantage of weekend, special and summer rates and packages. (See also ACCOMMODATION on p.118 and the list of RECOMMENDED HOTELS starting on p.65)

Meals and drinks. **Continental breakfast** in a restaurant/café costs 50Skr; **lunch** 60-70Skr; **dinner** at a medium-priced restaurant (not including drinks) 200Skr per head; coffee or soft drinks 15Skr; bottle of wine 100Skr and up; spirits (4cl) 70Skr, except aquavit (4cl) 50Skr. Like hotel breakfasts, lunch can be a good bet. Look for the sign *Dagensrätt* (dish of the day): salad, a main course and coffee.

Museums: 10-50Skr, average 30Skr. (Some are free.)

Petrol costs 7.70-8.10Skr per litre and diesel about 5.75Skr. Many petrol stations have automatic 24-h pumps, which take 100Skr notes.

Public transport: costs vary from place to place, but in Stockholm a single ticket for bus/*Tunnelbana*/local train is 13Skr.

Stockholm Tourist Card: Unlimited free travel on *Tunnelbana* and buses but no sightseeing concessions. Cost: 56Skr for 24 hours for journeys within the Greater Stockholm area; three-day ticket 107Skr. There are similar concessionary travel tickets, all sold at *Pressbyrån* (newspaper shops). Note: travel on Stockholm's buses is free for one parent if you have one or more children in a pram or pushchair.

Taxis: basic charge 45-70Skr within the city area. Some Stockholm taxis have a set fare of 75Skr within the Stockholm city boundaries.

Tourist City Cards: Stockholm, Gothenburg, and Malmö all have concessionary cards, with big savings on sightseeing, public transport and shopping, bought from tourist information centres.

Stockholmskort (Stockholm Card) gives free travel on local transport services (except airport), free city parking, sightseeing by coach and boat, and entry to many museums and main places of interest. A basic 24-hour card costs 150Skr, 72-hour card 450Skr. Gothenburg and Malmö have similar schemes.

All three cities offer **packages** which include accommodation at selected hotels, plus a 'Kort' (discount card), available mid-June to mid-August and at weekends throughout the year.

Trains: Single journey between Stockholm and Gothenburg, 2nd class 394Skr. Single sleeper journey, Stockholm–Kiruna 2nd class, rail ticket 594Skr plus sleeper 155-855Skr, depending on facilities.

Video: To rent a video camera 400Skr for 24 hours, plus MOMS. Cost of a 3-hour cassette tape 40Skr.

OPENING HOURS (See also PUBLIC HOLIDAYS on p.133)

Shops: weekday opening 9am-6pm; weekends 1pm-4pm. Some big stores and shopping centres in larger towns stay open until 8 or 10pm. In rural areas, closing times for shops and petrol stations is usually 5 or 6pm. Shops close early the day before a public holiday.

Banks: 9.30am-3pm; in larger cities some stay open until 5.30pm. Banks close on Saturday except for those at airports: Arlanda Airport daily 6.30am-10pm; Landvetter Airport Monday-Friday 8am-6pm, Saturday until 5pm, Sunday 12.30-8pm; Sturup Airport Monday-Friday 9am-3pm.

P

PHOTOGRAPHY (fotografering)

You can buy most makes of cameras in Sweden, including the superb Swedish Hasselblad brand. Colour films usually take three or four days to be developed, but in the cities many shops offer same-day or next-day services.

I'd like a film for this camera.	**Jag skulle vilja ha en film till den här kameran.**
black and white film	**svartvit film**
colour prints	**färgfilm**
132 colour slides	**färgfilm för diabilder**

How long will it take to develop (and print) this film?	**Hur lång tid tar det att framkalla (och göra kopior av) den här filmen?**

POLICE (*polis*) (See also EMERGENCIES on p.125)

Main Police stations are open 24 hours and have a public desk for incidents, thefts or other problems, and usually a local lost property office. Police patrols tour the streets and random car checks are more frequent than in many other countries.

The emergency police number (also fire, ambulance etc) is **90 000**; no money is required from a pay phone.

PUBLIC HOLIDAYS (*helgdag*)
(See also OPENING HOURS on p.132)

Banks, shops and offices close on the public holidays listed below, and may also close earlier the day before. Entertainment venues such as cinemas, museums and restaurants may stay open on some public holidays. The country grinds to a standstill on 24 December, the day Swedes celebrate Christmas.

Near Year's Day	*Nyårsdagen*	1 January
Twelfth Night	*Trettondagen*	6 January
Labour Day	*Första Maj*	1 May
Midsummer Day	*Midsommarsdagen*	Sat between 21 and 26 June
All Saints' Day	*Allhelgondagen*	Sat between 31 Oct and 6 Nov
Christmas Eve	*Julafton*	24 December
Christmas Day	*Juldagen*	25 December
Boxing Day	*Annandag jul*	26 December

Movable Dates

Good Friday	*Långfredagen*	late March/early April
Easter/Easter Monday	*Annandagpåsk*	late March/early April
Ascension Day	*Kristi himmelsfårdsdag*	May
Whit Monday	*Annandag pingst*	May

133

RELIGION

Around 95 percent of native Swedes are Lutheran, but there are also over 50,000 Roman Catholics, plus Jewish and other faiths. Numbers of Muslims have grown with immigration, but still account for only a small proportion of the population. Lutheran and other churches are listed in telephone directories and *Malmö This Month*.

TIME DIFFERENCES

Sweden keeps Central European Time, one hour ahead of Greenwich Mean Time. Clocks go forward by one hour during the summer (late March to late September). This differs in duration from British Summer Time and can cause some confusion with airline schedules, etc.

New York	London	Paris	**Stockholm**	Sydney	Auckland
6am	11am	noon	**noon**	8pm	10pm

TIPPING

Egalitarian Sweden is not a tipping nation. Service charges are included in bills, but it is usual to round up the restaurant bill to the nearest 10Skr. It is not necessary to leave a tip for the chambermaid.

Taxi drivers do not normally expect a tip, but it is customary to round up the fare to the nearest 10Skr. Add 10 percent if, for example, the driver carries a case up a flight of stairs. When you leave a coat in a cloakroom, the charge is usually 7Skr per article.

TOURIST OFFICES

Sweden is divided into 24 regional tourist organizations, and there are some 300 tourist offices in total. All have a selection of brochures, leaflets and maps of their respective areas.

The Sweden Travel Shop occupies the same building as the Stockholm Information Centre (Sweden House) and has a wide selection of information on regions other than Stockholm, plus a similar advice and booking service. On the upper floors in Sweden House are the Swedish Institute's library and its excellent bookshop.

Tourist offices (*turistbyrer*) are marked with the international tourist sign (white 'i' on green background) and in season are very busy. The staff answer questions, help with (and book) accommodation and tours, and often have typical Swedish goods on sale.

Stockholm Information Service (including other sections in Sweden House), Sverigehuset, Kungsträdgården, Box 7542, S-103-93 Stockholm; tel. (0) 8-789-20-00.

Gothenburg Tourist Office, Kungsportsplatsen 2, S-411-10 Göteborg; tel. (0) 31-10-07-40.

Malmö Tourist Office, Skeppsbron 2, S-211-20 Malmö; tel. (0) 40-30-01-50.

Swedish Travel and Tourism Council, Arenavägen 41, Box 101-34, S-121-28 Stockholm; tel. (0) 8-725-55-00.

OVERSEAS OFFICES

Great Britain: Swedish Travel & Tourism Council, 73 Welbeck Street, London W1M 8AN; tel. 0891-200-280.

USA: Swedish Tourist Board, 655 Third Avenue, 18th floor, New York NY 10017; tel. 212-949-23-33.

TRANSPORT

Sweden has good and well-maintained bus and rail services. Long distances make domestic airlines important. Cities and larger towns are linked by SAS, Transwede and City Air Scandinavia.

Buses (*bussar*). Swebus operates express bus services between larger towns in Southern and Central Sweden and between Stockholm and the northern coastal towns. There are also weekend-only services on main routes. A postal bus network operates in the north.

In cities buses are frequent, comprehensive, and well integrated with other transport. Stockholm's bus network is the largest in the world, run by the Stockholm Transit Authority, which also operates **135** integrated underground and local train services. Gothenburg has an ecologically friendly tram network.

Trains (*tåg*). The network run by Swedish State Railways (SJ) covers the whole country, with new X2000 high-speed trains cutting times on Stockholm–Gothenburg and Stockholm–Karlstad trips. Long-distance trains have restaurant cars and/or buffets, and there are also sleepers and couchettes for both first and second class.

The *reslustkort* (wanderlust card) offers half-price, second-class travel on certain trains, and other cost-cutting benefits. It is valid for one year, costs 250Skr, and is good value. On some trains, marked 'R' or 'IC', you must reserve a seat (price 20Skr), which can be done right up to the time of departure.

Inlandsbanen (Inland Railway), a special scenic line, runs from Mora in Dalarna to Gällivare beyond the Arctic Circle. *Wildmarksexpressen* (the Wilderness Express) has old 1930s coaches with a gourmet restaurant, and runs on the same line between Östersund and Gällivare, with stops and excursions (see p.91). Further details are available from Inlandståget AB, Kyrkagatan 56, S-831-34 Östersund; tel. (0) 63-12-76-92.

Full-fare tickets can be bought outside Sweden free of VAT, which is charged on tickets bought in Sweden. Ask at travel agents.

Taxis (*taxi*). Taxi ranks are marked *taxi*, but you can also hail taxis on the street. A lit sign, *Ledig*, means a taxi is free. You can also book by phone: look under *Gula Sidorna* in the telephone directory for numbers. Taxis have meters and willingly issue receipts; overcharging is not usually a problem.

Underground (*tunnelbana*). Stockholm Transit Authority runs the underground, *Tunnelbana* or *T-banen*, which covers 95km (60 miles) of track and incorporates 100 stations. These are marked with a large 'T', are very clean, and have been nicknamed the 'world's largest art exhibition', because of specially commissioned artwork in many of them. Stockholm also runs a good system of local trains.

Ferries and Boats (*färja; båt*). Despite its many waterways and large lakes, more often ferries connect Sweden to other countries rather than linking it internally. Many islands have regular connections, one of the busiest ports being the Baltic island of Gotland (see pp.50-1). There are also tourist boats in and around the Stockholm archipelago and in other coastal areas, in addition to regular services. Big lakes, such as Vänern, Vättern, Mälaren, Siljan, Storsjön and others, also have services.

The Göta Kanal (see p.60) is a classic pleasure route for Swedes and visitors alike. Details of canal trips are available from Rederi AB Göta Canal, Hotellplatsen 2, Box 272, S-401-24 Göteborg; tel. (0) 31-80-63-15.

TRAVELLERS WITH DISABILITIES

Facilities for disabled people include access ramps, lifts, and hotel rooms adapted for people with mobility difficulties or allergies, good public transport access, and special provisions for swimming and riding. Almost all pedestrian crossings use sound to indicate when it is safe to cross. For further information contact Sweden's National Council for the Disabled: Statens Handikapprådd, Regeringsgatan 567, S-103-96 Stockholm; tel. (0) 8-787-73-20.

TRAVELLING TO SWEDEN

Air: Scandinavia's flag carrier, SAS, most main European, and several North American airlines fly into Stockholm's Arlanda Airport. SAS, Transwede, City Air Scandinavia and a few smaller operators offer internal connections to all parts of the country. Gothenburg's Landvetter and Malmö's Sturup airports have some international flights and also connections to the internal network.

Sea: from Britain, Scandinavian Seaways sails Harwich–Gothenburg throughout the year and Newcastle–Gothenburg in the summer. From Continental Europe, the main routes are Kiel–Gothenburg, Travemünde–Trelleborg or Travemünde–Malmö. From Denmark: Frederikshavn–Gothenburg, Helsingør–Helsingborg, Dragor–Malmö and Copenhagen–Malmö. The bridge between Denmark and Sweden will provide a direct car route. There are also services between Stockholm and Helsinki, Russia, and the Baltic States.

Rail: the main Continental cities are linked to Sweden by rail. From London (Victoria) either via Dover and Ostend, or from London (Liverpool Street) via Harwich and Hook of Holland. From London it is also possible to travel (with your car) in *Le Shuttle* channel tunnel to Paris, from where you can continue your journey by road.

Alternatively, the Harwich–Esbjerg ferry or in summer the Newcastle–Esbjerg ferry (Scandinavian Seaways), connects with a train to Sweden via Copenhagen.

Coach: many countries are connected to Sweden by coach. London to Stockholm, via Amsterdam, is cheap, but takes over 40 hours.

W

WATER
Sweden's water can be safely drunk from the tap, but Swedes also favour bottled water, and the local *Ramlösa* is on sale everywhere.

WEIGHTS and MEASURES (See also DRIVING on p.123)
Sweden uses the metric system. Weather temperatures are given in degrees Celsius (named after the Swede who invented the system).

WOMEN TRAVELLERS

Relationships between men and women in Sweden are probably the most 'equal' in the world, and Swedish women organize their own lives freely, enjoying themselves as and when they please.

There are many women's organizations, mostly connected to political parties, but two professional (rather than social) ones are:

Stiftelsen Kvinnor Kan, Östermalmsgatan 33, S-114-26 Stockholm; tel. (0) 8-723-07-07.

Yrkeskvinnors Riksförbund (Federation of Business and Professional Women), Drottninggatan 59 3tr, S-11-21 Stockholm. It is affiliated to the International Federation of Business and Professional Women.

Y

YOUTH HOSTELS (Vandrarhem)

Sweden has 280 youth hostels (over 100 open year-round) in a range of buildings from manor houses and former prisons (Långholmen in Stockholm) to purpose-built. Many lie in remote areas as well as towns and cater for all ages, with two- and four-bed, and family rooms. All have self-catering facilities, and some also serve meals.

Hostels are run by Svenska Turistföreningen (Swedish Tourist Club), who offer everything from camping packages and simple mountain cabins, where you bring your own food, to hotel-standard accommodation, as well as operating small boat harbours and advising about cycling holidays and cycle hire.

Members of other countries' hostel associations qualify for cheap rates if they can produce their membership cards. The normal price is 60-90Skr per night, plus 35Skr for non-members. You should provide sheets or sheet sleeping bags but can also buy or hire them.

In summer, book ahead as this form of holiday is very popular. Further details and a list of hostels (price 59Skr, plus postage for youth hostel members, 69Skr for non-members) is available from: STF, Box 25, S-101-20 Stockholm; tel. (0) 8-790-32-50. Details can also be found in the International Youth Hostel Handbook.

Index

Where there is more than one set of references, the one in **bold** refers to the main entry, the one in *italics* to an illustration. (**Note**: in Swedish, å, ä and ö are the last three letters of the alphabet.)

143

Berlitz – pack the world in your pocket!

Africa
Algeria
Kenya
Morocco
South Africa
Tunisia

Asia, Middle East
China
Egypt
Hong Kong
India
Indonesia
Japan
Jerusalem
Malaysia
Singapore
Sri Lanka
Taiwan
Thailand

Australasia
Australia
New Zealand
Sydney

Austria, Switzerland
Austrian Tyrol
Switzerland
Vienna

Belgium, The Netherlands
Amsterdam
Brussels

British Isles
Channel Islands
Dublin
Ireland
London
Scotland

Caribbean, Latin America
Bahamas
Bermuda
Cancún and Cozumel
Caribbean
French West Indies
Jamaica
Mexico

Mexico City/Acapulco
Puerto Rico
Rio de Janeiro
Southern Caribbean
Virgin Islands

Central and Eastern Europe
Budapest
Hungary
Moscow and St Petersburg
Prague

France
Brittany
Châteaux of the Loire
Côte d'Azur
Dordogne
Euro Disney Resort
France
Normandy
Paris
Provence

Germany
Berlin
Munich
Rhine Valley

Greece, Cyprus and Turkey
Athens
Corfu
Crete
Cyprus
Greek Islands
Istanbul
Rhodes
Turkey

Italy and Malta
Florence
Italy
Malta
Naples
Rome
Sicily
Venice

North America
Alaska Cruise Guide
Boston

California
Canada
Florida
Greater Miami
Hawaii
Los Angeles
Montreal
New Orleans
New York
San Francisco
Toronto
USA
Walt Disney World and Orlando
Washington

Portugal
Algarve
Lisbon
Madeira

Scandinavia
Copenhagen
Helsinki
Oslo and Bergen
Stockholm
Sweden

Spain
Barcelona
Canary Islands
Costa Blanca
Costa Brava
Costa del Sol
Costa Dorada and Barcelona
Costa Dorada and Tarragona
Ibiza and Formentera
Madrid
Mallorca and Menorca
Seville

IN PREPARATION
Disneyland and the Theme Parks of Southern California
Milan and the Italian Lakes